D0992162

09/23
STRAND PRICE
FOR $5.00 EACH

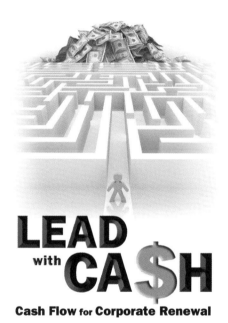

# LEAD
with
# CA$H

**Cash Flow for Corporate Renewal**

# LEAD
## with CA$H

## Cash Flow for Corporate Renewal

Harlan Platt (Northeastern University, USA)

Imperial College Press

ICP

*Published by*

Imperial College Press
57 Shelton Street
Covent Garden
London WC2H 9HE

*Distributed by*

World Scientific Publishing Co. Pte. Ltd.
5 Toh Tuck Link, Singapore 596224
*USA office:* 27 Warren Street, Suite 401-402, Hackensack, NJ 07601
*UK office:* 57 Shelton Street, Covent Garden, London WC2H 9HE

**British Library Cataloguing-in-Publication Data**
A catalogue record for this book is available from the British Library.

**LEAD WITH CASH**
**Cash Flow for Corporate Renewal**

ISBN-13 978-1-84816-375-1
ISBN-10 1-84816-375-4

Typeset by Stallion Press
Email: enquiries@stallionpress.com

Printed in Singapore by Mainland Press Pte Ltd.

# Contents

# 1. Introduction

As I write this, the world economy is in the midst of a nearly unprecedented slowdown. Some have called it the Great Recession, while others have more boldly deemed it the 21st-Century Depression. Whatever it is called, the devastation of wealth, emotional well-being, and aggregate national output has been startling. Companies once thought to be giants have failed, such as Lehman Brothers, Bear Stearns, Chrysler, and General Motors. Others such as Merrill Lynch and Wachovia Bank have been absorbed by healthier competitors. AIG, once an insurance behemoth with a trillion dollars in assets, is now operating under government conservatorship. Less well-known victims of the devastation that litter the corporate landscape are equally noteworthy: Circuit City, Extended Stay Hotels, Six Flags, and Trump Entertainment Resorts Inc.

*Lead with Cash* has been written in the hope that its message can bring better management to other companies, enabling them to avoid failure during good times and bad. The message in *Lead with Cash* — an onomatopoetic phrase, for the words give the entire meaning — is unique. This book instructs the reader on how to lead a company in a new way: by focusing entirely on cash and cash flow. Ideas presented here are, for the most part, not included in the "normal" lexicon of management tools; no one else preaches the idea that cash is the only metric, and that everything else is secondary.

I have structured the book in a counterintuitive style. There are three parts. Part I describes specific thoughts on how management should be conducted with cash as the focal point. Part II contains chapters that explain what cash flow is, how it is calculated, and alternate definitions of cash flow. Part III contains observations and insights from a group of turnaround and restructuring professionals who have utilized various parts of the *Lead with Cash* message in their work. Short biographies of each contributor appear at the end of Part III.

Some readers may prefer to start with Part II and then proceed to Part I. I have taken the liberty of creating this unorthodox structure to get the conceptual ideas of *Lead with Cash* across to readers before the details and minutiae of cash flow chase them away. I think that the ideas in Parts I and III are most important. Readers who learn the essentials of managing with cash by reading Parts I and III but who are not comfortable with accounting aspects of cash flow calculation will gain most of the benefits.

What is important is that all readers learn the message of *Lead with Cash*, and that all companies begin to manage themselves by considering how every action and every deed affects their cash flow.

# PART I

# 2. Lead with Cash: Achieve Great Results by Identifying the Right Target

A man walked into his office one day and found a team of movers carrying out his desk. "Where are you going with that?" he screamed. A tall guy with tattoos and a shaved head smirked at him and replied, "The new owners are auctioning everything off." "What new owners?" the man asked, "I thought I could work out my company's troubles."

The fictitious scenario depicted above can befall any business. Today your company is successful. Tomorrow it is gone. Chaotic change is rampant and its effects are pervasive. Few companies fail, but many others undergo rapid sales declines and a loss in profitability. The survivors may eventually perish too unless they learn to manage their business better. Your business is at risk unless you fix it! The furniture movers, in the metaphor above, may not walk out with your company's computers tomorrow, but be assured that your competitors are actively trying to steal your customers today. Management styles from even a few years ago are anachronistic. Today's situation demands a new approach, a more inclusive business model. The task of survival must be transmitted throughout the organization. Everyone must participate if your company is going to survive.

Not long ago, unhealthy companies traveled a longer and safer path. This path had numerous perpendicular branches that led to safety. The course that companies follow today is shorter and more dangerous. An unhealthy company's descent once began by the company getting sick, then consulting a number of different doctors (turnaround agents), and finally with it entering a hospice setting (bankruptcy court). However, things have changed. Sympathetic creditors willing to compromise and forgive are figments of the past. Today's credit adversary is likely to be a hardnosed, Ivy League-trained MBA who carries a BlackBerry and two cell phones and who cares very little about the human cost of corporate death. Lost jobs, ruined communities, and wiped out stockholders matter little to these wizards of Wall Street.

Sudden corporate demise afflicts large and small companies alike. Size alone is not a safety net. Longevity is no defense. When a company finds itself in trouble, it must either quickly find a path to recovery or it will vanish. Living in a fast-paced world has many advantages that improve the way we live, but it also destroys the value of financial relationships and business friendships. You can no longer walk down the street to the local bank and talk with someone who attends your church and lives in your neighborhood. Companies fail today because of what they did yesterday. Creditors are probably investors who bought the loan from a distressed bank or hedge fund and are only interested in making a quick dollar. The number of steps leading up to the guillotine is very small compared to historic times when companies had greater power to renegotiate terms with lenders, who wanted companies to survive so long as they received waiver fees and a small boost in the interest rate they earned.

The key to survival in the new world is to lead with cash flow. Cash flow is the target. Everything a company does should be aimed at improving its cash flow. The first principle in finance, one that every business student learns like a mantra, is that the value of a firm equals the current value of its future cash flows. Cash flow is a company's life blood. Everybody who works in an organization needs to understand what cash flow is and, more importantly, how to manage their part of the business with an eye on cash flow. By making decisions that improve cash flow, you keep your creditors from having anything to say about your company's future. Creditors have never been known for being compassionate, but now they have become downright avaricious. They are as willing to pull the rug out from under a company as they are to put sugar in their coffee. The key to survival is to stay out of the clutches of creditors. Moreover, the key to successful growth, as opposed to growth that actually leads to trouble, is to grow cash flow. Companies and their managers and employees need to learn what cash flow is, and how to manage the organization while making constant reference to how things impact cash flow.

This book teaches both of these goals. It provides a primer on cash flow that virtually every employee can benefit from. Then, it creates the ideology that all companies, but especially those feeling the brunt of a competitor's actions, need to be managed with a constant focus on cash flow. What a crazy juxtaposition! Cash flow management coupled with more productive workers. Cash flow management coupled with more innovation. Cash flow management coupled with happier workers. That is the future envisioned in *Lead with Cash*.

How come no one ever thought of this before? They have. Many successful companies have been practicing leadership with cash flow. Most of these companies are family-owned businesses for whom cash flow determines whether their kids get braces, whether their spouse gets a new car, and whether the family prospers. The vast majority of companies know what cash flow is and what management is; they just have not learned to put the two concepts together. These companies overlook the benefit of interjecting cash flow throughout the enterprise. Companies actually locate cash flow specialists on one floor and then conduct management activities elsewhere in the building. At the end of the quarter, the cash flow experts figure out whether the company's cash flow has grown or shrunk and then they retreat back into their cash flow hiding place. Other employees may learn about the quarterly cash flow, but they do not think about how their own actions can affect cash flow. This book changes all that. *Lead with Cash* provides a framework to help companies get off the old way of managing and onto the new wave.

# 3. Name the Team
# "Cash and More Cash"

It is impossible to exaggerate what can be done with focus and concentration. People, organizations, and companies can all achieve great things if they apply a concerted focus to their goals. Look at the remarkable opening ceremony that China presented at the 2008 Summer Olympics featuring 15,000 performers in a four-hour extravaganza. Few will ever forget the spectacle. For centuries, Eastern philosophers and others have taught those wishing to achieve enlightenment how to focus themselves in order to achieve inner harmony. *Lead with Cash* advocates a similar dialectic for businesses. Companies need to focus their employees on the target. Notice I didn't say "a target" but instead "the target", by which I mean cash.

## Getting Everyone to Focus on Cash

A great day at the office seems to end too soon. You are kept busy doing things you like to do and time just evaporates. Imagine that everyone in your company has a job which fits that description. They come to work, get a lot done, and actually enjoy themselves. Now ask yourself whether those employees, at some point during the day, have thought about maximizing the company's cash flow. The answer is probably not. This tells us two things: (1) cash and cash flow are not uppermost on people's minds, and (2) the way to affect cash flow is by designing jobs so that improvement in cash flow is a natural or automatic outcome of the job.

If a job is well thought out and properly designed, the busy worker in the paragraph above is actually improving the company's cash flow daily as he or she performs his or her tasks. Most workers do not understand their contribution to cash flow. This is true unless managers include cash flow education as part of a regular process of information exchange with their team. This general lack of knowledge raises an intriguing question: should employees be taught about cash flow or can the same goal be accomplished by redesigning jobs so that they "automatically" improve cash flow? The answer to this question is the subject of *Lead with Cash*. In brief, cash flow should be taught and retaught, but jobs should be designed to emphasize the need to protect and bolster the company's cash flow. Unless everyone focuses on cash flow, it gradually fades into the background and is soon lost amid the noise of daily activity — making sales, buying supplies, hiring workers, etc. When that happens, jobs lose their attachment to cash flow and take on a life and purpose of their own.

Patriotism is a similar phenomenon to focusing on cash flow. Most Americans — as they make their way through school, religious education, and parental guidance — become reasonably patriotic. This patriotism comes out when the national anthem is played, while walking down Constitution Avenue in Washington, D.C., and during times of geopolitical stress. On a daily basis, however, it gets buried beneath concerns about jobs, family, and sports teams. True, the individual is still patriotic, but he or she does not think about it and it does not affect their job, family, or sports team. The difference between patriotism and focusing on corporate cash is that patriotism does little to help most individuals in their job, with their family, and in the sports arena; in contrast, focusing on cash flow actually helps companies. That is why companies are advised to educate their workforce about how strong cash flow increases the company's liquidity, enables new investment in productive facilities, and ultimately, if things go according to plan, may culminate in higher wages or bonuses for all.

Companies can help their employees to think more about cash by following three simple steps. First, they need to insist that managers regularly clarify or decode, for their employees, the relationship between their job and the company's cash flow. Second, they need to regularly report to employees what has happened to corporate cash flow. Finally, they should establish a reward system that benefits the individual worker when cash flow achieves a pre-set goal. The operative words are **Clarify, Report, and Reward**. Every manager should have a checklist with "clarify, report, and reward" on his or her desk as a constant reminder to keep channeling information to the team.

The first task, clarifying how the job affects corporate cash flow, is the most critical and the most difficult. It is critical because it is the nuts and bolts of the entire "lead with cash" process. If managers fail to translate how each job affects cash flow and how cash flow affects the firm, then the worker will focus on satisfying personal needs and not those of the company. Workers, for example, may be more concerned about leaving their desk before the rush hour or hiring workers locally, even though better workers can be hired, with more effort, in the neighboring town. Sure, they still get their job done, but the company's cash flow would improve if they put aside their personal desires and focused on the company's needs. One strategy is to relate individual salaries and benefits to the accomplishment of company-wide cash flow goals. Let workers know what will happen if company-wide cash flow does or does not increase.

The rapid change in jobs and job descriptions is what makes the interpreting task so difficult. On top of that, people are constantly changing jobs within the same company. Managers, too, may lose sight of cash flow if the jobs in their domain are constantly changing. This is not to say that the job does not get done; rather, my point is that in such a situation it is the manager's or the worker's interests that are preeminent and not the company's.

The second task of reporting to workers is accomplished in a variety of ways because of worker variability. Among their differences are that some workers are highly educated, while others are not; some are permanent employees with decades-long affiliations with the company, while others are newly hired; and some workers are paid straight salaries, while others receive salaries plus a bonus. This diversity problem is resolved by bifurcating information so that all workers learn about items which change cash flow, while only some

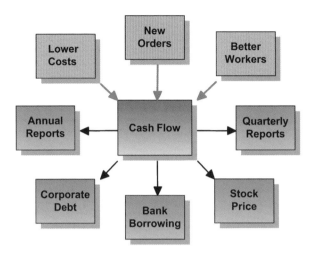

Fig. 3.1   The Cash Flow Information Transmission System.

workers are given information about things affected by cash flow. Of course, no one should ever be denied information about cash flow. This demarcation merely stresses that some workers benefit more from detouring around cash flow itself to things that affect cash flow. Figure 3.1 helps to illustrate this point.

The figure has three parts. In the middle is cash flow itself. On the top of the figure, with vertical lines running through the boxes and gray arrows running to the center, are items affecting cash flow. At the bottom of the figure, in solid boxes with black arrows coming to them, are items that cash flow affects. All workers should be informed about the items on the top of the figure; everyone needs to know, for example, about new orders received or customers lost. Workers on a day-to-day basis are connected to order reception, and it is a small step between that and cash flow. Getting a new order is an accomplishment that requires the input of many people and which improves cash flow. Everyone's morale is helped by seeing what their hard work has achieved. More sophisticated workers and those opting to be fully informed should also receive the information at the bottom of the figure. Annual and quarterly reports should be emailed to everyone signing up for them or employed in certain departments; more detailed reports on items like changes in bank or other borrowings should be judiciously emailed to this same group of workers[1]; and for public companies, it is not a bad idea to have boards displayed in various locations containing information about changes in the company's stock price.

The third task is the most enjoyable. Rewarding employees for cash flow accomplishments is not the same thing as setting wages and benefits; those are derived through other mechanisms. Cash flow rewarding is about saying thank you. The rewards do not have to be big, nor must they be small. For example, if a goal of reaching $1 million in cash flow is established and after hard work throughout the organization a company accomplishes that goal, the company might hold a small event or give out a corporate gift costing about $2,500. Workers wearing the gift shirt or cap, or using the gift pen, or sitting in the grandstand at the local Class AAA baseball game know why they are there, provided that their managers have done a good job in the first task of explaining the relationship of their job to the company's cash flow.

Competition is usually beneficial, but the benefits of competition do not extend to cash flow education. Focusing on cash flow does not benefit from competition. It is a team effort that requires everyone to pull together to accomplish a goal that is good for each. When the system is working, one department is encouraging another and each is concerned about the outcomes of all.

## Task 1: Deciphering the Cash Flow Relationship

Every part of a business has its own specific target: human resources wants to decrease employee turnover, purchasing wants to reduce costs, marketing wants to maximize the number of new customers, and so on. I call these local targets. But the main target — and there should only be one for the whole business — is cash. Maximizing the company's cash flow should be the responsibility of every employee.

---

[1]Legal counsel may require this information to be distributed publicly at the same time, which might alter which information is distributed.

In order to do this, employees need to work to achieve their local targets. Local targets are critical to achieving the main target. Unless all players on the team work to achieve their local targets, the main target cannot be reached.

Think of the many targets within a company as being similar to the various roads on a map. Most roads get you from here to there, but the main road takes you somewhere important. Yet, local roads are necessary. The main road cannot function without local roads. A town with only local roads is cut off from the rest of society. A town with only a main road has traffic passing through it, but local residents are cut off from the outside world. While local roads are critical to the functioning of a transportation system, the main road is the real highlight of the grid. Failure of a local road creates problems; failure of the main road creates havoc.

Similar to the transportation analogy above, local targets within a company are important. They direct employees to achieve key goals that benefit the entire organization. The main target, though, is what really matters. To understand the relative correspondence between local and main targets, consider the unlikely event that a company is successful in hitting its local targets but unsuccessful with its main target. The outcome would be unsatisfactory. Yes, everyone is doing their job, but the company is lagging. What has probably happened in this case is that local targets have been set incorrectly, without respect to cash flow. Redefining local targets can revitalize and refocus the enterprise.

Good local targets have one common characteristic: they direct the company towards its main target. The main target is cash. Of course, local targets may not articulate a cash-based goal and the workers listening to them may not understand cash-based directions, but the ultimate motivation expressed in a local target must be cash flow. Most employees have never heard about the connection between their unit's goals (local target) and cash flow. Those companies are not part of the "lead with cash" movement. Employees need to understand that local targets are critical to the mission of the company. No matter what task they do, their performance contributes to the company's success or failure.

Human resources, for example, may have a local target of decreasing employee turnover. Purchasing may want to reduce the costs of purchases. Marketing may be trying to get new customers. Why are they aiming at these local targets? The answer is not "because that is our job." The *Lead with Cash* answer is "because if we do so, the company will generate more cash and I know that cash flow helps the company."

Specific units within a company get their own targets or goals so that employees know what to do. Imagine walking into the human resources, purchasing, or marketing department and saying, "OK, what I want you to do today is to maximize the company's cash flow." Employees would nod their heads in agreement and give you a round of rousing applause when you leave, but they would not know what to do. Local goals establish a work plan for employees in every unit so that they clearly understand what their job entails.

The task of the manager is to articulate local unit targets that employees can understand, fully support, and put into operation. Ultimately, though, the targets must circle back to company cash flow. Managers who fail to understand this should not be managers. An additional task for the manager is to help employees see how the local targets relate back to the main target. This task need not be difficult, nor does it have to be too technical. Each manager should work to get his or her team to coalesce around the unit's targets, and to help workers understand how the company's cash flow is improved when the unit hits its target.

For example, the CEO has told the human resources (HR) manager that the company's cash flow would improve if it could reduce employee turnover, hire higher-skilled workers, and increase rank-and-file morale. The manager begins by telling the HR team that they have three unit goals. The manager specifies these goals, saying that during the next year employee turnover needs to be reduced by 10 percent without changing wages or benefits, worker skill levels need to rise by 15 percent based on a specific test, and a survey of morale that the company conducts each year needs to improve by 20 percent. The manager then asks the team to devise a plan to achieve the unit's targets. During that process, he or she educates the team on how accomplishing each of the three targets results in improved corporate cash flow. He or she also realizes that education is a continuous portion of his or her job, since (1) most of the team is vague on what cash flow is; and (2) like everyone else, team members are more concerned about their own work level, compensation, and possibly the unit targets than any corporate goals. By educating the team about cash flow, how it affects the company, and how unit targets relate to corporate cash flow, the manager creates a workforce that improves the unit's success and thereby helps corporate cash flow.

## Task 2: Reporting Cash Flow

Cash flow information can be either good or bad news. Companies are advised not to participate in the dangerous game of reporting only one type of cash flow news. Some companies report only good news; others report only bad news. Instead of picking and choosing what to dispense, all news should be communicated and explained where necessary.

The school of thought which only supplies good news is not a wise approach. Generally, companies taking this tack either have bad managers who are trying to insulate themselves from the consequences of their poor performance or who believe that workers respond best to positive signals. Bad managers should be removed; that is a given. Only telling employees about good news may be a sign of bad managers. The best way to persuade these individuals to report all cash flow news, and not just the good news, is by instilling in them a strong sense of camaraderie with the rest of the team. Like Captain Ernest Shackleton, who commanded a dispirited crew of 26 sailors lost on an iceberg in Antarctica in 1914, the way to salvation is through teamwork, problem solving, and finally celebrating victories together.[2]

---

[2]See, for example, Jennifer Armstrong, *Shipwreck at the Bottom of the World*, Crown Books for Young Readers, New York, 2000.

Managers who think that only bad cash flow news should be discussed as a way to encourage even greater performance are also misled in their thinking. Teams that are successful need to be informed of their success; everyone likes to be praised. Sure, talking about what is not working helps workers to reexamine what they are doing and helps them to seek out better solutions. But to omit good news or to cover it over with less important bad news is dangerous. Workers see through this charade and stop listening. Like the story we tell our children about "The Boy Who Cried Wolf", this is a futile effort that will surely backfire and hurt the "lead with cash" effort.

## Task 3: Rewarding Cash Flow

Remember when a parent came home and brought you a small inconsequential gift as a reward for doing a chore at home extra well? It probably came out of the blue and caught you completely by surprise. I do not want to get into any child-rearing controversy, but present the example because it or something similar has probably happened to most readers. What is important is how this parental gift affects behavior. The essential seven questions are these:

(1) After receiving the gift, did you do the next chore better than usual?
(2) If you knew in advance that you were likely to get the gift, did it encourage you to do the task especially well?
(3) Had you known a gift was in store if you did a good job, would you still have done a good job?
(4) If you had been expecting the gift and you did a really great job on the task but your parent forgot to get you a gift, would it have made you angry and less productive in the future?
(5) After receiving the gift, did you get angry when after completing the next chore you did not get a gift?
(6) If your sibling slacked off and did a poor job on a similar task and then did not receive a gift, did this encourage you to continue to be a good worker?

(7) If your sibling slacked off and did a poor job on a similar task yet despite that he or she still received a gift, did this discourage and reduce your performance on the next task?

Since each person is unique, everyone answers these seven questions somewhat differently, and of course there are no right answers. But let us consider them carefully. Remember that the gift itself is inconsequential, maybe a comic book or a trip to the local ice cream store. The first question asks whether your future behavior changed following the gift. Certainly if you had been given $1 million you would have raked the yard better than anyone else ever has, but all you got was a $1 comic book. Most people would have appreciated the gift and its acknowledgment of good work; they would probably modify their future behavior and do a better job than usual. Some people might have said, "It's just a lousy comic book, I'm not going to work that hard again!", but they are in the minority.

The second question concerns anticipation. Some workers will push themselves hard to ensure that their team gets a company baseball cap or a coupon for a free doughnut. Others are less persuaded by simple gifts. If the camaraderie I spoke about earlier takes hold, more workers will feel the excitement of working to achieve a cash flow goal for which they will receive a $1 gift. Readers may wish to explore the behavioral economics literature to understand how and why people make irrational choices. An example of an irrational choice would be a worker who earns $23 an hour putting in an extra hour at work so that each member of the team can get the $1 coffee coupon.

Question 3 asks whether knowledge that the company had a plan to reward workers with an inexpensive gift if a cash flow goal was met might somehow reduce the worker's performance. In fact, I take the opposite view. People do not want to let others down, which includes teammates and the company itself. Advance warning that a gift could be earned should stimulate greater effort.

The fourth question is asked as a warning to companies. If workers expect a little acknowledgment for their hard efforts and the gift is withheld, then future behavior may be impacted. It would be an irrational response to not work as hard since they did not receive a baseball cap, but that is how the human mind works. Do not advertise or promote a plan and then abandon it. While you may not think that a pizza party after work is very important, the workers who heard you promise it certainly do. Do not make promises that you do not intend to keep. Either workers will decide that the promise-maker is unreliable, or they may even jump to the erroneous conclusion that the company is in trouble and is not spending the few dollars to protect cash flow. You do not want either message to go out.

Question 5 asks whether once a gifting program is begun it is necessary to perpetuate it. The answer is of course not, if you only plan on a single gift and then make that fact known upfront. On the other hand, if the pre-announcement of a gift helped in some small way to get the firm to its cash flow goal, doesn't it make sense to continue the program? I think so.

The last two questions are discussed together. There is no doubt that people look over their shoulder at their neighbor. That is where the expression "keeping up with the Joneses" came from. The biblical commandment to not covet your neighbor's possessions is partly a response to this human tendency to compare oneself with others. If rewards are given out, they should not be bestowed on units or people who did not meet expectations. Doing that makes the entire program a joke. In fact, knowing that some unit was not rewarded may help to motivate a good team in the future. They may want to avoid being labeled as shirkers or nonperformers themselves.[3]

Clarify, report, and reward are the three ingredients needed to "lead with cash". They help educate workers on how what they are doing also affects company cash flow and ultimately their own compensation; they update workers on progress being made toward goals; and they say "thank you" in a very low-cost way. Is it worth the effort? I think so. I firmly believe that a company can improve its overall performance and make itself a better place to work by following the advice in *Lead with Cash*.

---

[3]This is not the type of competitive behavior that I already spoke against. The worker does not want the other team to fail, but seeing that they are not rewarded when they do fail may encourage them to continue to work hard.

## Good to Great

Jim Collins' *Good to Great* has been a very successful book since it was published in 2001.[4] Recently, some analysts have questioned his methodology and have pointed out that many of his 11 "great" companies have not prospered in the intervening years. I am not concerned about that. I would simply like readers to observe how his plan for achieving greatness, which he defines as beating the financial performance of peers by several multiples, begins with an approach not too different from our objective in this chapter.

I argue that companies must focus their organizations on the main target, which is cash flow. Like me, Collins says that the process of achieving greatness begins by "getting the right people on the bus" and then figuring out where to take the bus. He is right: hire good workers and then get them all to pull in the same direction. Where I differ from *Good to Great* is in what the target ought to be. Collins believes that companies should use "the hedgehog concept", that is, companies should do those things that propel their economic engine (I have argued that this is cash flow) and what they are best at and most passionate about. I, on the other hand, believe that companies should do things that increase their cash flow in the foreseeable future. I leave it to managers to determine what those things are.

Collins actually comes closest to saying what *Lead with Cash* says when he tells companies to narrow their focus and stick with what they are good at. This should have a familiar ring by now: do not do things that do not contribute to discounted cash flow (DCF). Companies that branch out, like the ice cream example in Chapter 5, had better be careful that they are moving in a direction which increases cash flow and not one which destroys cash flow. Focus and core competence are examples of systems that help companies avoid diverting their attention to new products and services at the expense of what they are good at doing.

---

[4] Jim Collins, *Good to Great: Why Some Companies Make the Leap . . . and Others Don't*, HarperBusiness, New York, 2001.

# 4. Rationalize Costs Focusing on Cash

Tom Brady of the New England Patriots is an expensive American football player. In May 2005, he signed a six-year contract extension that pays him US$60 million through 2010. But Tom's list of accomplishments is also prodigious: he made four Super Bowl appearances and won three Super Bowl victories between the 2001 and 2007 seasons; he holds the NFL record for most touchdown passes in a season and the NFL record for most consecutive team victories; and *Sports Illustrated* named him Sportsman of the Year in 2005. Weighing these achievements against his salary, it is unclear whether Tom Brady is an expensive football player or not.[1]

The issue is not whether US$60 million (or US$10 million a year) is a lot of money. Sure it is. The question is how to compare the US$60 million against Tom Brady's game performance and the associated revenues earned by the New England Patriots organization. I imagine that some wealthy team owners do not view their team roster salary discussions with a "lead with cash" analytical approach. But most of those teams are underperformers. Their owners should read *Moneyball: The Art of Winning an Unfair Game* by Michael Lewis,[2] which tells the story of how the lowly Oakland Athletics can consistently field a winning team on a skimpy budget. Other examples of sports

---

[1] Tom's injury in the first game of the 2008 season notwithstanding, he is still one of the greatest football players in history.

[2] Michael Lewis, *Moneyball: The Art of Winning an Unfair Game*, W. W. Norton & Co., New York, 2003.

teams that are not "lead with cash"-managed include the New York Yankees and the Washington Redskins, which perennially have one of the highest salaries in their respective professional sports leagues (baseball and football) yet consistently fail to win. What matters is not how much you pay an athlete, but how much you get for what you pay. This truism applies to sports teams, businesses, and families.

A good example of the "be sure to get what you pay for" thesis is found in the non-business topic of gastric bypass surgery. This type of surgery is given to obese individuals and basically involves reducing their capacity to eat by artificially shrinking their stomachs. Bariatric surgery costs approximately US$26,000 per case while laparoscopic surgery, a less invasive treatment, costs approximately US$17,000. Ignoring issues of self-esteem and appearance, the benefits of the surgery are improved health and well-being for the patients. Many obese individuals have hypertension, diabetes, high cholesterol, or other major ailments. The reduction in weight resulting from the surgery has been shown to alleviate or reduce the impact of these ailments on some surgery recipients. A study in 2008 showed that the surgery's costs are recoverable (by paying fewer subsequent medical bills) in as few as 25 months.[3] Thereafter, medical insurers and employers are positive net beneficiaries. Not surprisingly, many insurance companies now agree to cover the cost of gastric bypass surgery. They are using the "lead with cash" mentality.

It is hard for a company not being managed in the "lead with cash" style to judge whether it is getting its money's worth from purchases. Undoubtedly the company knows how much each item costs and what each is supposed to deliver, but most companies fail to stay on top of purchases after the product has been delivered. Therefore, they are unable to fully evaluate their purchases in the "lead with cash" framework. In the gastric bypass surgery example above, unless hospitals and doctors kept records of illnesses, hospital stays, and medical office visits subsequent to the surgeries, it would not be possible to make a strong affirmative statement about the surgery.

---

[3]See Rhonda L. Rundle, "Obesity Surgery Is Called Cost-Effective," *The Wall Street Journal*, September 8, 2008.

You might think that an inability to judge whether your firm's purchases are justified by the quality, quantity, or nature of their use is a small issue, but you would be wrong. Not getting their money's worth is a major problem for companies. Suppose that just 10 percent of what companies spend each year is wasted or poorly allocated. In the aggregate, that would amount to a loss or wasted expenditure by American businesses in excess of US$1 trillion.

How do companies rationalize costs focusing on cash? The answer is fairly straightforward. They begin by estimating how and to what extent a purchase benefits the company; then, that benefit estimate is compared against the total cost of the purchase. Somehow this seems too simple. You would expect that companies already do this. But, in fact, most companies do not because (1) few companies quantify how a purchase benefits them, and instead they say "we need it" or "it's time to replace it"; and (2) by "costs" I mean total or true costs, and not just the upfront purchase price of an item. Benefits or costs that occur many years in the future must be discounted to determine their current value.[4]

When a company has rationalized costs focusing on cash, each purchase the company makes results in an increase in its cash. Unless it can be shown that a purchase is cash-positive (i.e., it increases the company's cash), the purchase should not be made. Deviations from this rule should require a careful review by the CEO or his or her designee and, for large purchases, should get approval from the board of directors. For example, a company may want to make an anonymous donation of cash or goods to charity. The benefits from that donation specific to the firm are few and the costs are high. This alone is reason enough to discourage the donation, but the board of directors may feel that the donation is necessary and appropriate. In that case, the rule can be relaxed.[5]

---

[4]Discounting is discussed in Chapter 10.

[5]I apologize to charities and their supporters for identifying them as a possible corporate purchase that might not pass the "rationalize costs focusing on cash" test.

Rationalizing costs focusing on cash begins by requiring a formal statement of expected benefits for every purchase. Employees may initially grumble that things are already too bureaucratic and that their time is being wasted. I agree with them, but these are necessary costs that must be paid to keep from wasting the company's cash. Benefits need to be articulated as well as accurately valued. I do not think this should be difficult. If a company or its managers cannot produce these estimates every time they want to make a purchase, I wonder why that company is buying new equipment, taking out an advertisement in a newspaper, hiring extra workers, etc. Employees must learn that, before they request a purchase, they need to vigilantly identify and quantify how that purchase benefits the company.

The method also requires a company to have a full understanding of the actual costs associated with a purchase. I do not mean just the cost of buying the item. What I mean is similar to the discussion you may have had with your son about buying his own car. He says, "I can buy it for just US$2,500. Please let me do it." To this plea you probably responded, "Well, in addition to that cost, each year you will have to pay about US$1,000 for car insurance, US$750 for repairs, and US$750 for gasoline." In other words, the purchase price is only about 50 percent of the ownership cost for the first year, and the non-capital costs continue every year that the car is owned by your son. The same is true of corporate purchases. There is the outright cost of making a purchase, and then there are the secondary and related costs that arise after the original purchase is made. Companies need to get the full picture about costs from their employees before authorizing a purchase; they need to know the item's true or total costs.

Undoubtedly, devious employees can discover ways to undermine this method. For example, they might provide misleading statements about expected benefits and purposely understate future costs. This problem can be mitigated by educating employees about the importance of cash to the company and thus indirectly to themselves. I recommend that one individual or one team of people make all the purchase decisions within a company, thereby forcing everyone to adhere to the same rules. On the one hand, spreading purchasing authority across disparate departments or groups fosters an environment that asks employees to fabricate their inputs. This is counterproductive and must be avoided. On the other hand, putting all this authority into one person's or group's hands creates a power structure that might not be healthy. One solution to this concern is to rotate qualified people into that role. Not only would this reduce the power held by the team, but it would also educate others within the company about the decision-making process.

After the benefits and costs are identified, the manager then merely needs to compare the one with the other. Normally, only purchases that result in an increase in cash are made. Deviations from this rule may occur when unknown benefits may exist or when it is believed that certain costs may ultimately be avoidable. While this introduces subjectivity into the analysis, it also creates an opportunity for good management and leadership. What it avoids, I hope, are large-scale purchases made without any reference to how they will affect the company's cash.

As a simple example, suppose a company has three choices regarding which laptop computers its sales people should use in the coming year. Choice 1 is to have the sales team continue to use their $2\frac{1}{2}$-year-old laptops. Choice 2 is to buy a great new machine from the top vendor for US$1,400 apiece. Choice 3 has the company buying a laptop from another less reputable manufacturer for US$900 apiece. Table 4.1 lays out the key characteristics of the three choices.

The cheapest decision would be to do nothing, but the head of sales says that her team is complaining that the older machines are unreliable, plus they are overweight and very slow in downloading

Table 4.1    Characteristics of Three Laptop Computer Choices.

| Choice/ Characteristic | Choice 1 — Use Old Machine | Choice 2 — Buy from Top Vendor | Choice 3 — Buy from New Vendor |
|---|---|---|---|
| Cost | US$0 | US$1,400 | US$900 |
| Speed | Slow | Blazing Fast | Blazing Fast |
| Weight | Heavier | Light | Light |
| Reliability | Falling | High | Unknown |
| Full Warranty | $\frac{1}{2}$ Year Remaining | 3 Years | 3 Years |

from and uploading to the Internet. Comparing between the two new machines, their technical specifications are identical; where the products differ is in terms of cost and reliability. The top vendor charges a premium because its brand is well established. The new vendor offers a less expensive alternative. However, the new vendor's machine is untested by the company and is not well documented by other users either. Both machines offer three-year full parts and labor warranties, and the new vendor has outsourced its repair activities to a well-known and reliable national computer service company. In other words, there should be no service difference between the vendors.

In most companies, the decision would be made by a person in the IT department. This is logical because that group is most familiar with computer brands, employee needs, and the firm's technological limitations and strengths. On the other hand, the IT person may not follow the "lead with cash" mantra. She probably has a mixed bag of interests and needs, which include the following:

(1) She wants to quickly resolve this request from the sales department.
(2) She wants machines that perform with few failures, if any.
(3) She wants to stay within her budget.
(4) She wants machines that require the least amount of technological support.
(5) She wants an easy ordering process.

On all five counts, the IT department's person is likely to select a new computer from the top vendor as the provider of choice, provided that the budget has been set high enough to accommodate the US$1,400-per-machine price. Since an IT person or someone very similar is usually part of the planning process, the budget will normally accommodate a high-priced bid from a well-known and often-selected vendor. After making the high-priced choice, the manager expects to leave the office every day at 5 pm and does not expect to receive emergency phone calls on the weekend. She has met her personal needs while fulfilling her job, but she may have spent more money than required.

Who else might be given the role of choosing between the three laptops? Perhaps the decision should be made by the company's chief financial officer (CFO) or the head of the sales department? They each have their own set of interests and needs, just like those of the IT department person. The CFO might, if the firm has had a bad year, prefer to focus on costs. She would therefore choose to not replace the older laptop. If the firm has had a good year, the CFO might nonetheless try to economize and might choose to buy the machines from the new vendor. After all, repair and education are responsibilities of the IT department and not finance. However, if the cheaper machine performs well, the CFO will get no praise; if they are massively unreliable, she will be criticized. For that reason, she may select the high-priced vendor against her better judgment. In that case, I argue that the company has not devised a purchasing system that protects employees to encourage them to make the optimal choice for the firm.

The head of the sales department, if given responsibility for this decision, is probably motivated to try to satisfy the needs articulated by her department. Her people are tired of lugging around heavy, unreliable machines. She will probably suggest buying from the top vendor. After all, cost is unimportant to her. Again, this outcome suggests a firm with a flawed purchasing system. How different would her choice be if her own compensation was tied to the department's costs or profits? In that case, she might choose to either do nothing or buy the cheaper machines. But if she works at a firm not engaged by the "lead with cash" concept, she may buy the name brand computer.

I cannot say without further information which laptop computer this hypothetical company should purchase. The choice depends on (1) an impartial assessment of the deficiencies of the currently employed machines and (2) the future reliability of the cheaper computer relative to the name brand computer. An honest dialog between the sales and IT departments, with both groups recognizing the company's needs for cash generation, will produce a fair assessment. Company policies can foster this type of interchange provided that adherence to the rules results in (1) no losers and (2) the company as the winner. Also, the IT department should be able to judge the new vendor's future performance, with some degree of error, by talking directly with the supplier and their current customers.

Let us suppose that a committee of sales and IT personnel agree that new machines are needed. The first choice of doing nothing and

Table 4.2   Analytical Framework to Compare Costs of Two Laptop Computer Brands.

| | Purchase Cost | Annual Cost of Broken Machines | 3-Year Cost of Broken Machines | Total Cost |
|---|---|---|---|---|
| Name Brand Computer | US$1,400 | US$600 | US$1,800 | US$3,200 |
| Off-Brand Computer | US$ 900 | US$660 | US$1,980 | US$2,880 |
| Savings with the Off-Brand | | | | US$ 320 |

keeping the older computers is therefore dropped from consideration. Also, the IT department estimates that laptops from the cheaper vendor would be 10 percent less reliable than from the best-selling vendor. The data on reliability can be easily misunderstood. It does not mean that 10 percent of the less expensive computers will not work. What it does mean is that if the name brand computer is expected to function perfectly except for 2 days a year, the off-brand model would have 2.2 down days per year. The head of sales estimates that a day without a laptop will cost the company approximately US$300. The new computer is expected to be retained for three years. The purchase decision can then be analyzed with this additional information as shown in Table 4.2.

Note that discounting, which reduces future expenditures to their current values, is not employed in the table, since the number of years is relatively small and the difference between values is relatively large. This choice keeps the analysis simple.

After including an estimate of the cost associated with incremental breakdowns of the off-brand computer, that brand still retains a 10-percent ownership cost advantage calculated over the three-year expected life span of the machines. This analysis holds everything else equal. The machines are technologically identical, have identical repair warranties and service, and will deliver the same computer power. In other words, the choices made earlier by the IT person, the CFO, and the head of sales were all wrong. To "lead with cash", the company should purchase the less expensive computer.

The basic idea is that costs — whether they are for low-cost items like ballpoint pens or expensive items like factories — need to be evaluated in terms of how they affect the firm's cash flow. Obviously, small expenditures do not require a major, rigorous analytical process before they can be authorized. But if employees became engaged by the "lead with cash" idea, they would bring that philosophy to even the smallest purchase. What this means is that the purchasing manager will stop buying more expensive pens, coffee cups, etc. while making sure, on her own, that the replacement items are of a sufficiently high quality to meet the actual needs of the company and its employees.

# 5. Make Product Decisions Based on Cash

Companies regularly make decisions about products.[1] Some decisions are for old/existing products and others are for new products. Many of these issues impact the company's cash as they affect the amount of cash spent or the revenues generated by specific products. Most companies do not target the cash implications of their decisions when engaged in these deliberations, but rather they ask questions such as:

- "How do we keep up with the competition?"
- "How do we grow revenue?"
- "What tweak do we give the product to make it appear new or better?"

These questions are all appropriate, of course, and should be asked. Most business people, at one time or another, have asked them. But notice how these questions are oblivious to either cash flow or profits. That is because most businesses are accustomed to making product decisions without reference to cash. And that is wrong!

---

[1] This discussion of products may seem to ignore plant (where the product/service is made), people (who make the product), and process (how it is made) issues, but this is not my intention. The reader may wish to read Harlan Platt's *Principles of Corporate Renewal* (University of Michigan Press, Ann Arbor, MI, 2004), which directly addresses the simultaneity between products, plants, processes, and people. Here, it is suggested that the reader extrapolate product decisions described in the text to plants, people, and processes.

Remaining competitive, growing revenues, and maintaining customer loyalty are all important corporate concerns, of course, but they should not be addressed independently of how these actions affect the company's cash. When companies violate this basic principle, they are asking for trouble. The need to consider products within a cash framework applies to old and new products alike.

Suppose, instead of the questions asked above, these very similar questions were asked:

- "How do we keep up with the competition **while growing our cash**?"
- "How do we grow revenue **and cash flow**?"
- "What tweak do we give the product to make it appear new or better **and therefore yield a higher cash flow**?"

The difference between the two sets of questions is minor in words but monumental in fact. What really matters is not which theoretical questions are asked, but how employees think and act. The objective of *Lead with Cash* is to teach companies and their employees to put cash considerations into everything they do.

Consider Table 5.1, which presents representative questions affecting new and old products. Each of these complex decisions should be approached systematically within a decision-making process that includes cash considerations. This is discussed below. But the truly important contribution of *Lead with Cash* is how cash needs to be a critical part of that decision-making process.

Table 5.1    Examples of Product-Level Decisions for New and Old Products.

| Decision | Legacy Product | New Product |
| --- | --- | --- |
| Introduce a product | | √ |
| Increase the marketing budget | √ | √ |
| Sell in a new market | √ | √ |
| Discontinue a product | √ | |
| Make a product platform addition | √ | |
| Modify a product to increase its appeal | √ | |

√ indicates that the decision includes that category.

Product decisions for existing products differ from new product decisions. With older products, companies might consider product repositioning (moving the product along the price or quality metric), product line extensions (adding a related product, e.g., a chocolate oat cereal), and product revisions (modifying characteristics, e.g., adding a larger hard drive to an MP3 player). But do repositioning, extension, and revision make sense for the company? Should the product be left alone or abandoned instead? No doubt whatever is produced by a repositioning, extension, or revision will be attractive and beautifully packaged, and will sit nicely on the store and customer's shelf. But will the company benefit? At the end of the day, the way to know if repositioning, extension, and revision benefit the company is by estimating cash flow. Yet many companies decide to undertake this type of project without including cash as a consideration! I suspect that, in these cases, an agency-type problem may result in decisions that are in the best interest of the employees but not of the company.

There are two types of new products: those that are new to the company (other companies are already in the market) and unique products that no one else offers. Introducing a copycat product, which is new to this company but which is available from other firms, is the less risky alternative since the choices made by established companies can be reviewed and their best decisions replicated. It may even be possible to hire someone who either originated or ran an existing firm's operations for a similar product. But even copying a competitor's offering is fraught with dangers when the company has little experience in this new product space.

Unique product decisions, when there is no one else to imitate, are more worrisome (cost- and profit-wise) than decisions made on existing or copycat new products since they involve new investments, markets, technologies, and supply relationships. Given the company's lack of experience with the new product, the venture is more risky and certain to have less accurate sales and profit forecasts. Moreover, since the product is new, the company has fewer existing resources that can be shifted to it. So, especially with unique new products, the focus of analysis should be on the cash implication for the company.

A major complication arises for companies considering a new product when they already have a related, existing product in their portfolio. An example of this issue is an ice cream manufacturer who is thinking about adding a line of packaged puddings. Do not confuse this situation with a product line extension: with a product line extension, the ice cream firm might add a line of frozen yogurts; pudding products, however, are not in the same category as ice cream and thus are a new product. The complication is (1) should the new product be introduced and the related product dropped, or (2) should both products be on the market simultaneously?

This question has a thousand answers, and no doubt everybody working at the ice cream company has his/her own opinion of what to do. Suppose we know the following additional information: ice cream is a marginally profitable and sometimes unprofitable business, while research suggests that pudding will be massively profitable over time if care is taken in how it is made and introduced. Figure 5.1 illustrates the expected cash flow from the two products.

The key driver in this and all corporate decisions should be cash flow. While the cash flow from ice cream is low, the product may require little further investment. That is, the manufacturing facility is built and operating, the formulae and supplier relationships

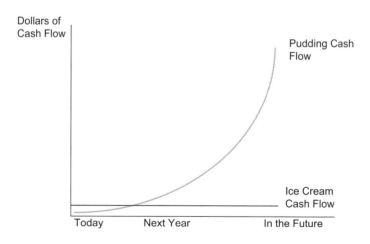

Fig. 5.1    Comparison of Cash Flow from Pudding and Ice Cream (over time).

are in place, and the distribution channel is established.[2] These are all advantages. In that case, the low cash flow from ice cream may be worthwhile maintaining. Of course, if a strategic buyer offered to take the enterprise for a high price, the company may be better off selling the ice cream division. On the other hand, pudding may require a large investment in facilities, contracting, marketing, and distribution. These are disadvantages.

The correct methodology to analyze the pudding/ice cream conundrum (and most other corporate decisions) is to use a cash perspective to compare the required cash outlay (let us call it the investment) to the present discounted value of future cash flows. This is called the discounted cash flow (DCF) method. Discounting is a way to equate future cash flows with current ones. Obviously you would prefer to receive a dollar today versus a dollar in 10 years, but what about receiving $1.43 in 10 years versus $1.00 today? The DCF method determines (using a discount rate based on the firm's cost of capital) today's value of future cash flows. By comparing the sum of all future cash flows to the dollar size of the investment (e.g., to introduce new products or to renew an old product), it is possible to evaluate whether an investment is worth pursuing.

The DCF method is demonstrated using data in Table 5.2 from the ice cream company to describe how it can use cash to decide about adding a pudding line. Let us assume that the company will need to make a further investment of $50,000 to continue making ice cream. It expects to have an annual cash flow from ice cream of $5,000. Notice that Table 5.2 only goes out four years. It is common in business forecasting to make specific and highly detailed projections about near-term years that are relatively easy to project, and then to condense all years beyond the near term into what is called the terminal value. The terminal value is calculated using the formula below:

$$\text{Terminal value} = \frac{\text{cash flow in the next subsequent year}}{(\text{cost of capital} - \text{growth rate})},$$

---

[2]Products like this are sometimes called "cash cows", though given the low profit level of ice cream a cow is perhaps too large an animal.

Table 5.2   Company Data on Ice Cream and Pudding.

|  | Investment | Cash Flow | | | |
|---|---|---|---|---|---|
|  |  | Year 1 | Year 2 | Year 3 | Year 4 |
| Ice cream | $ 50,000 | $ 5,000 | $ 5,000 | $ 5,000 | $ 5,000 |
| Pudding | $1,000,000 | $ 20,000 | $200,000 | $500,000 | $600,000 |
| Discount factor |  | 0.91 | 0.83 | 0.75 | 0.68 |
| *Discounted cash flow* |  |  |  |  |  |
| Ice cream |  | $ 4,545 | $ 4,132 | $ 3,757 | $ 3,415 |
| Pudding |  | $ 18,182 | $165,289 | $375,657 | $409,808 |
| *Discounted terminal value* |  |  |  |  |  |
| Ice cream |  |  |  |  | $   34,151 |
| Pudding |  |  |  |  | $15,114,839 |
| *Discounted total value* |  |  |  |  |  |
| Ice cream | $   50,000 |  |  |  |  |
| Pudding | $16,083,776 |  |  |  |  |

where cost of capital (assumed to be 10 percent in this example) measures the firm's capital cost across all of its sources of money (equity, debt, preferred stock, etc.) and growth rate is the estimate of how rapidly cash flows will increase beyond the forecast years. The terminal value is discounted back to the current year.

In the example above, ice cream cash flows are assumed to have zero growth (as is true during the four-year forecast period); while pudding cash flows are assumed to grow at 8 percent, which is far below the expectation of the first four-year pudding forecast, making this a conservative assumption. Any investment which has a present discounted value of future cash flows that is greater than the investment amount is a good investment. This produces a simple decision rule about when to proceed with a project:

Discounted total value > discounted investment cost.

Sometimes a project returns more undiscounted cash flows than the cost of the investment, but after discounting future cash flows are less than the investment cost:

Discounted total value < discounted investment cost.

Those projects should be abandoned since their discounted cash flow return is less than the investment cost. In other words, the firm cannot earn its cost of capital on the project. You might say that the company would be better off putting its money into the bank!

The pudding concept requires an upfront investment of $1,000,000. Some people at the company might attack the pudding concept by comparing the large investment negatively against the smaller, $50,000, investment required to stay in the ice cream business. But when the future cash flows are discounted, the pudding investment is expected to return a present discounted value in excess of $16,000,000. In other words, after accounting for the time value of money by discounting future cash flows, the pudding idea is tremendously successful: it is expected to return 16 discounted dollars for each dollar invested (be aware that few actual investments are this good).

The $50,000 ice cream investment would allow the company to redesign the packaging on its half-gallon containers. The new design has generated great excitement in various quarters of the enterprise, the CEO has agreed that the new packaging is better than the old one and possibly better than competitors', and a panel of ice cream eaters has endorsed the design. The company would probably go forward with the concept, except that it has begun to "lead with cash". Looking at the DCF analysis above, the CEO correctly decides not to make the investment in a packaging redesign for the ice cream business. Consider the logic of spending $50,000 now to earn $50,000 in the future discounted to present values. The company would do better by putting its money into a bank and not investing the $50,000.

The $1,000,000 pudding investment would require the company to dig deep and find new sources of capital, perhaps by establishing a $500,000 credit line with its bank and taking out a $500,000 loan from its board of directors. Throughout the company, dissenting opinions are heard arguing that:

- "We are an ice cream company. What do we know about pudding?"
- "We might lose some ice cream customers to our pudding."
- "The $1,000,000 could be better spent on more redesign efforts on the ice cream brand."

The company might have succumbed to the pressure of shrill voices, except that it had begun to "lead with cash". A $1,000,000 investment that returns $16,000,000 after discounting is a big winner in the "lead with cash" world.

Having decided to invest in pudding still leaves unresolved the question of whether the ice cream product line should be kept or abandoned. The ice cream company would not be the first firm to change gears and enter a new market. For example, F.W. Woolworth Company, one of the original five-and-dime companies, left its core business when that appeared to have little future. The company transitioned over to become Foot Locker, Inc. because management guessed correctly that athletic shoes would be a more profitable, cash-driven product in the future. In another classic case of leaving the past behind, GE today makes the majority of its cash flow from its finance businesses; it left light bulbs far behind.

If we relax the earlier assumption that the ice cream business requires a $50,000 investment and instead assume that the business can operate with no further investment, then the ice cream business is cash-positive from a DCF perspective. Despite this, the company may still wish to exit the ice cream business if its managers believe that they will not have sufficient time to run both an ice cream and a pudding business. If instead a $50,000 investment is in fact needed to receive future cash flows, the ice cream business would be abandoned.

Questions other than those discussed above should also be modeled and evaluated with the DCF method. For example, should the company increase the promotion on its products by spending more on advertising? This is an example of a common question that most businesses ask regularly. Of course, disciplines like marketing, accounting, market research, logistics, and strategy have important contributions to make to these discussions. I am not arguing that their inputs should be neglected and only DCF be relied on. Rather, my point is that the *key* decision variable in all product decisions must be the impact the decision has on cash and cash flow. There is little gained in having the newest and shiniest product on the street if your firm runs out of cash and goes bankrupt.

Before making a product decision, new or old, a company's managers should review information about product design (whether it is fresh or old), product engineering (how, where, and with what it is made), and market analysis (market size, market share held, potential increase in market share, and the product's price point). With a new product, the slate is clean but, as mentioned above, it is harder to get the numbers right. With existing products, most of this information is known and understood. However, an additional factor that must be considered is the product's life cycle and strategies to maintain the product.

## Product Life Cycle

Ray Vernon developed the idea of product life cycles in 1966.[3] It has since become a critical way to think about a business' products. The

---

[3]See Ray Vernon, "International Investment and International Trade in the Product Cycle," *Quarterly Journal of Economics*, Vol. 80, 1966, pp. 190–207.

idea is that products go through life phases similar to what an individual experiences. The basic model suggests that products have four life phases: birth, adolescence, maturity, and end. During the birth phase, the product is identified, demand is stimulated by advertising, profits may be negative due to low sales volume and high costs, and the market may have few competitors. In the adolescence phase, the product achieves profitability, scale effects push down costs, and competition arises. Maturity brings lower prices and product differentiation as companies fight to maintain their market share. Profits may begin to wane during this period. Finally, in the end phase, sales decline, costs increase, and profits become elusive. The four phases are represented in Fig. 5.2.

I have already discussed how the DCF method should be used in the birth phase to help make new product decisions. The technique is also highly relevant during the adolescence, maturity, and end phases. The reason why product decisions after the birth phase also benefit from a DCF framework analysis is that not every product experiences the nice curvilinear phases depicted in Fig. 5.2. Unfortunately, some products die along curves B or C as shown in Fig. 5.3. These products were introduced, presumably after a DCF analysis using the best data available found the product to be a good risk. Then, something went amiss; perhaps a strong unexpected competitor emerged or maybe the product failed to live up to its potential. In any case, the products on curves B and C died an early death.

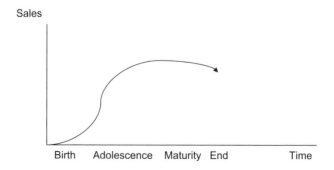

Fig. 5.2   The Normal Product Life Cycle.

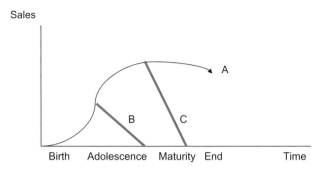

Fig. 5.3   The Alternative Product Life Cycle.

DCF analysis should be used to reassess products continually after their birth to ascertain that they continue to be good investments.

The product life cycle theory actually lends support to the basic argument for using DCF throughout a product's life. First, if products have a life cycle, then it must be the case that at some point the products will die. Second, if a life cycle exists, then product profitability varies over its life cycle. DCF can help decide whether a product is worthwhile holding onto or whether it should be allowed to die. The driver behind a DCF analysis is expected free cash flow (or the dollars available to the firm after paying for all the product's costs, including equipment maintenance), which is then compared to the new investment needed to maintain the product.

Consider the values in Table 5.3. The example describes a product that for some reason or other, perhaps a regulatory requirement or a geological reality, has a 10-year remaining potential life. The word "potential" conveys the fact that the company, if it subscribes to the "lead with cash" concept, is constantly deciding whether to continue or abandon the product. The table assumes, as was done earlier, a 10-percent discount rate to reduce future cash flows to their present value. Also, to reflect the impact of the maturity and end phases on corporate cash flows, as described in Fig. 5.2, it is assumed that annual cash flows decline throughout the period. The estimated free cash flows are all at their maximum values; that is, it is assumed that the company during the next 10 years will wisely make advertising,

Table 5.3    Required Investment Dollars and Expected Free Cash Flow for an Existing Product.

| Year in the Future | New Investment Dollars | Expected Free Cash Flow | Discount Factor |
|---|---|---|---|
| 1 | $0 | $350,000 | 0.91 |
| 2 | $0 | $318,182 | 0.83 |
| 3 | $0 | $262,960 | 0.75 |
| 4 | $1,000,000 | $197,566 | 0.68 |
| 5 | $0 | $134,940 | 0.62 |
| 6 | $0 | $ 83,787 | 0.56 |
| 7 | $0 | $ 47,296 | 0.51 |
| 8 | $0 | $ 24,270 | 0.47 |
| 9 | $1,000,000 | $ 11,322 | 0.42 |
| 10 | $0 | $  4,802 | 0.39 |

marketing, distribution, supply requisition, and other decisions to achieve the most from the product.

In the annual review, the CEO asks this key question: should we maintain this product, which has concluded its adolescence period and entered its maturity phase? As seen in Table 5.3, while a steady stream of cash flows is expected over the next 10 years, the product will require two investments, each for $1,000,000, in years 4 and 9. The DCF decision-making process produces a set of discounted investment dollars and free cash flows as seen in Table 5.4. At the bottom of the table are two net present value (NPV) calculations. The first determines the NPV (discounted revenues less discounted costs) of the product to the company for the first eight years (only the first $1,000,000 investment is made), while the second determines the NPV of the product throughout its entire 10-year potential life.

The positive NPV estimated for continuing the product for eight years contrasts sharply with the negative NPV for the product over a 10-year life. The CEO is likely to decide to make the first $1,000,000 investment and earn positive discounted net cash flows from the product for eight years, but then discontinue it as the need for the second investment nears.

Introducing DCF analysis to product-level decisions is important for all companies, but it is especially important for those companies

Table 5.4   Discounted Investment Dollars and Expected
Free Cash Flows for an Existing Product.

|  | Discounted New Investment Dollars | Discounted Expected Free Cash Flow |
|---|---|---|
|  | $0 | $ 318,182 |
|  | $0 | $ 262,960 |
|  | $0 | $ 197,566 |
|  | $683,013 | $ 134,940 |
|  | $0 | $ 83,787 |
|  | $0 | $ 47,296 |
|  | $0 | $ 24,270 |
|  | $0 | $ 11,322 |
|  | $424,098 | $ 4,802 |
|  | $0 | $ 1,851 |
| Total | $1,107,111 | $1,086,976 |

NPV through Year 8 = $397,310.
NPV through Year 10 = ($20,135).

that have adopted continuous product development (CPD). CPD is a good idea. It enables companies to maintain their edge and competitive advantage. However, without DCF controlling which CPD decisions are undertaken, the company is likely to find itself spending a great deal of money to make its products better but not achieving any financial reward for its efforts.

Consider the cash flows given in Table 5.5. The product development results in a minor (about 4-percent) increase in free cash flow, which over the 10 years aggregates to an additional $57,405 of free cash flow. The discounted cost of the investment (not shown in the table) is $910,000. In this case, while the product development makes the product thinner, sharper, or more appealing, it does not carry its weight in terms of generating new free cash flow. The innovation should not be undertaken.

An interesting issue arises when a product development will "save" the business from being stolen by a competitor but not yield any extra cash flow. You can hear the managers now: "We have to do it, otherwise we will be out of business." This statement may be true,

Table 5.5    Incremental Dollars of Free Cash Flows from a Product Development.

| Year in the Future | New Investment Dollars | Expected Free Cash Flow Without the Investment | Expected Free Cash Flow With the Investment |
|---|---|---|---|
| 1 | $1,000,000 | $ 350,000 | $ 364,000 |
| 2 | $0 | $ 318,182 | $ 330,909 |
| 3 | $0 | $ 262,960 | $ 273,479 |
| 4 | $0 | $ 197,566 | $ 205,469 |
| 5 | $0 | $ 134,940 | $ 140,338 |
| 6 | $0 | $  83,787 | $  87,139 |
| 7 | $0 | $  47,296 | $  49,188 |
| 8 | $0 | $  24,270 | $  25,241 |
| 9 | $0 | $  11,322 | $  11,775 |
| 10 | $0 | $   4,802 | $   4,994 |
|  | Total | $1,435,125 | $1,492,530 |

Table 5.6    Incremental Dollars of Free Cash Flows from Another Product Development.

| Year in the Future | New Investment Dollars | Expected Free Cash Flow Without the Investment | Expected Free Cash Flow With the Investment |
|---|---|---|---|
| 1 | $1,000,000 | $0 | $ 350,000 |
| 2 | $0 | $0 | $ 318,182 |
| 3 | $0 | $0 | $ 262,960 |
| 4 | $0 | $0 | $ 197,566 |
| 5 | $0 | $0 | $ 134,940 |
| 6 | $0 | $0 | $  83,787 |
| 7 | $0 | $0 | $  47,296 |
| 8 | $0 | $0 | $  24,270 |
| 9 | $0 | $0 | $  11,322 |
| 10 | $0 | $0 | $   4,802 |
|  | Total | $0 | $1,435,125 |

but unless the expenditure can be justified by cash flows it must not be made. This situation is demonstrated with the data in Table 5.6.

Just as the managers alleged, without making the incremental product development investment, the stream of free cash flows will plummet to zero. But by spending $1,000,000 (with a present discounted value of $910,000), the company can maintain its cash flows of $1,435,125 (with a present discounted value of $1,086,976). Since the discounted return exceeds the investment, the new development should be undertaken.

## Case Study[4]

Sony is a recognized world leader in quality electronics. Yet Sony has faced profit pressures. Sony has suffered in part from its inability to sell products to the lower half of the buying spectrum. It is not that those consumers do not want a great Sony product, but rather that they cannot afford to buy one. As a consequence of Sony's intransigence and insistence on quality, it has made room for other manufacturers, notably from other Asian countries, to make inroads into the electronics market. In fact, Vizio grabbed the lead and became the market leader for TVs in 2008.

Sony's liquid crystal display (LCD) TV line has been losing money for years. Imagine the prolonged silence that would have been heard when Sony engineers suggested creating a line of less expensive LCD TVs. Managers, when pressed for a decision, may have said something like, "The more TVs we sell, the more money we lose, so the answer is NO!" But Sony has a new CEO, Howard Stringer. Stringer had been President of CBS from 1988 to 1995, after which he was President at TELE-TV. During these stints, he became known as a turnaround manager, partly due to his management style of allowing divisional presidents to make autonomous decisions. He is also known for focusing a company on cash and cash flow.

What apparently happened at Sony is that managers were told they could compete with the cheaper TV offerings from other companies provided they did two things: (1) spend few dollars in development and (2) make a profit. To accomplish the first, the new

---

[4]This case study draws heavily upon Yukari Iwatani Kane, "Sony's Newest Display Is a Culture Shift: A Low Cost TV Shows the Way to Better Profits," *The Wall Street Journal*, March 8, 2008, p. B1.

TVs were created using parts and designs straight off the shelf. To achieve the second, the TVs were produced cost-effectively in Sony's Mexican factories and sold at competitive prices. While Sony does not reveal product-level profitability, we do know that the TVs were initially to be sold only at Wal-Mart stores but, because of their great success, they are now sold at Best Buy as well. Sony also acknowledged that the TVs are profitable.

Sony's success is also partly due to its effort to get managers in different divisions and areas of the world to communicate with each other. However, there can be no questioning the importance of Sony's adoption of a "lead with cash" mentality as also being a big catalyst for this improvement.

# 6. Set Strategy with Cash

Companies need to articulate a strategy and then follow it. That much is obvious. I could say that a company without a strategy is like a ship without a rudder, or a fine restaurant without a chef, or countless other appropriate expressions. Since there are good and bad strategies, merely having one does not guarantee success. Success requires a strategy that is right for the company and right for the times. I argue that to be right, a strategy must be "cash-aware". By "cash-aware", I mean that a strategy considers how it impacts the firm's cash flow.

Other authors have noted how a good strategy improves a firm's profitability and cash flow. My contribution to this discussion is that improving profitability or cash flow is not enough. A strategy must also be cognizant of the *annual* cash requirements and the *annual* cash flow contributions it may cause. Simply defining a strategy that may lead to the largest future cash flow out of all possible strategies ignores the choppy journey that a firm will travel as it implements a strategy.

Every year, firms must pay their bills. Debt holders, suppliers, and other creditors are never sympathetic to a firm that is late in making payments when the firm claims that its strategy, given a few more years, will lead to untold riches. Creditors look upon those claims much as you would view someone who is sitting beside you at a bar, sweating profusely, and imploring you to lend them money to invest in a "sure thing". Companies that do not pay their bills on time are put out of business before their dreams can be realized. The strategy yielding the highest future cash flows but resulting in failure in the short run is not the best strategy, even though it may, on paper, lead to the greatest fortune.

A strategy is a plan that describes how a company will achieve its goal.[1] Notice that I didn't say "make more profit" or "sell more widgets". Every company has its own internal goals. Too many companies have goals that are not based on a cash metric; rather, they target market share or possibly revenues. Some company goals are short-term goals, while others are long-term goals. In the abstract, neither time span is better than the other, since the company with the short-term goal may intend or need to sell itself in the near term and cannot wait for a long-term strategy to develop.

A business strategy should guide a firm to a position where it has a competitive advantage. As the words suggest, a competitive advantage allows a company to beat its competitors. The most common competitive advantages are cost advantage (being the low-cost provider) and differentiation advantage (e.g., differences in quality, location, or design). Most competitive advantages dissipate over time as competitors adapt and learn how to compete. Sustainable competitive advantages are rare and usually come from a valid patent, a first-mover advantage, or a resource constraint.

Some universal business strategies, and well-known companies that have adopted them and made them famous, are:

- Offer good products at great prices — e.g., Wal-Mart Stores, Inc.
- Be a great place at which to work — e.g., Whole Foods Market, Inc.
- Focus on the customer's needs and wants — e.g., Wynn Resorts Ltd.
- Lead with technological developments — e.g., Apple Inc.
- Achieve a commanding monopoly position — e.g., Microsoft Corporation.

---

[1]In contrast, a tactic is how things will be done immediately. Strategies may take years to play out.

Of course, any strategy can fail. Sometimes the failure of a strategy results from internal problems such as failure to implement the strategy properly, failure to coordinate between units of the business, or unwillingness among employees or managers to do things differently. Strategic failure can also occur from external causes such as misreading competitors' responses, what customers want, or the level and reliability of governmental support. Having a person or a team that is given authority to shepherd and care for a strategy may improve its likelihood of success. The need for individual attention from a change master is greatest when a significant transformation such as a strategic or cultural shift is involved. Of course, if the change master is not sufficiently empowered to push the new strategy throughout the organization, he or she will accomplish little.

## Porter's Competitive Strategy

Michael Porter has made contributions in numerous business disciplines. One of these is strategy.[2] Porter argues that a firm is strong either because it has low costs or because it has been able to differentiate itself from the rest of the pack. To achieve higher returns, firms should go with their strengths; that is, the low-cost firm should seek dominance by using price as its lever, while the differentiated firm succeeds by attracting discerning consumers to its product line. Porter's third strategic category is companies that focus on a narrow market segment rather than across an entire industry. The focused firm can opt to be either a low-cost provider or a differentiated one (see Fig. 6.1).

So that the reader does not get confused, I provide the following examples of broad and narrow scopes within the same industry. In the airline industry, Southwest Airlines Co. is a firm with a broad scope and low costs; while British Airways Plc, another firm with a broad scope, has a differentiated strategy offering ultra premium

---

[2]Michael E. Porter, *Competitive Strategy: Techniques for Analyzing Industries and Competitors*, The Free Press, New York, 1998.

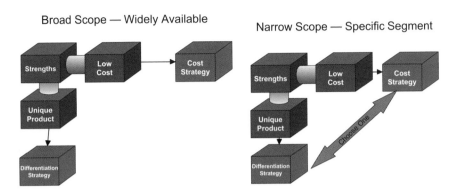

Fig. 6.1    Porter's Generic Strategies.

seating and other lavish perks for its business travelers. Other air carriers have focused strategies. For example, Mesa Air Group succeeds by being a low-cost feeder carrier for a number of legacy airlines including United Airlines (UAL Corporation), US Airways Group, and Delta Air Lines; while Cape Air shuttles wealthy travelers to luxury locations. Both Mesa Air Group and Cape Air can succeed despite their small size and limited resources; airlines do not have to be monoliths like British Airways. Similarly, Southwest Airlines can compete with British Airways as a result of its low-cost structure.

Companies do not just decide to be a cost leader. Cost leadership generally comes as a result of either a natural or scientific fact that a company controls or influences. Examples of these are patents (which provide 17 years of exclusive use), special resources such as favorable ore deposits in a mine, or operating efficiencies resulting from sharp business decisions. Sometimes cost leadership can be gained by consolidating an industry and thereby achieving economies of scale that cannot be matched by other firms. Having cost leadership does not mean that a company can forsake quality, since some consumers may prefer a higher cost alternative that delivers more of another attribute. In commodity markets, however, price and low cost may be the only factors that matter.

Before attempting to differentiate its products, a company should engage in a careful analysis of its market and consumers to determine which product/service attributes will attract a sufficient volume of sales and a high enough price to make the investment worthwhile. By targeting these desirable features, a company can hope to attract a segment of a market to its offering. Risks to this strategy are that consumer tastes and preferences may change, or that another company has reached an identical conclusion and is planning to enter that market too. General Motors and Ford, which made billions of dollars selling large, fuel-inefficient sport utility vehicles (SUVs), painfully found out about changing consumer tastes when gasoline prices reached record levels in 2008. At the same time, Honda Motors gained market share and profits by differentiating itself from other auto manufacturers by focusing on fuel efficiency and safety.

Focusing on or picking a small segment of an industry to sell in is also a winning strategy. Offering a small segment of the population a special product that is unavailable elsewhere may create a lasting profitable relationship between consumers and the firm. Good examples of this are Tom's of Maine dental products and Whole Foods Market, Inc., which caters to health-conscious consumers. Sometimes the narrow focus strategy can become so successful that it leads to a broad strategy. For example, Apple began by selling computers that appealed to design- and image-centric users, but then, as other consumers gradually learned about the other qualities of its products, its market penetration gradually increased. White Castle Management Co. has succeeded with low-cost hamburgers, which attract budget-conscious consumers away from giants such as McDonald's or Burger King. Its burgers now have an almost cult-like status among aficionados.

## Porter's Five Forces

Another Michael Porter contribution to the products literature provides a way to evaluate strategy. He called this development the five forces.[3] The five forces are:

- The threat of entry by a competitor;

---

[3]Michael E. Porter, *Competitive Advantage*, The Free Press, New York, 1985.

- The intensity of intra-industry rivalries;
- The availability of substitutes;
- The power of buyers to extract lower prices; and
- The power of suppliers to raise costs.

A positive outcome for the five forces is often a result of strategic decisions. Companies with limited potential of entry from new competitors usually control some aspect of the production process, perhaps with a patent, or have a commanding economy of scale which frightens away other firms. Strategically, this is a firm possessing cost leadership. When the intensity of intra-industry rivalry is low, it is often the case that the industry has a number of differentiated competitors, each of which is comfortable in its own niche. In other words, vibrant, healthy companies are created when industry participants make strategic choices to differentiate themselves. Not having to worry about substitute products, perhaps for technological or legal reasons, allows a firm to artificially act like a pseudo-cost leader. There is no doubt that picking the right sector in which to compete, as a strategic choice, profoundly affects a company's health. Finally, a company with weak customers and suppliers may benefit from a decision to differentiate itself from other producers. When there is a single provider of a critical product, buyers are weakened. It is hard for customers to bargain for a price concession or improved quality if there are no other producers offering similar products. When a firm can choose from among numerous suppliers, it gains power. Competition between suppliers, as Porter suggests, benefits a company.

The connection between strategy and Porter's five forces and corporate health is clear. As illustrated in Fig. 6.2, when each of the five forces aligns with the company, the firm is likely to be healthy with strong profits.

## Product Families and Strategy

More recently, observers have recommended that companies pursue product platforms as a way to obtain cost leadership, differentiation,

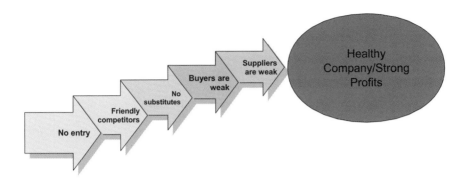

Fig. 6.2   Alignment of the Five Forces.

or both.[4] A product platform creates a family of products based upon an original idea by redesigning the product to serve a variety of needs and markets. In other words, it is a strategy that creates differentiation within an individual company. An example of this is Apple, which has taken the basic iPod product and expanded it to include tiny products such as the iPod Nano (in a multitude of colors), iPod Shuffle, and iPod Touch which adds Internet connectivity. Apple is relentless in continuously pursuing additions to its product platform. What makes product platforms especially important is that the cost of adding products to a platform is low relative to the cost of a newly developed product. Moreover, when a company has a reputation for product platforms, competitors are reluctant to enter their marketplace. Product platforms raise the barrier to entry.

## Product Portfolios

Few companies rely on only a single product. Most businesses operate with a portfolio of products. Sometimes the portfolio is held at a single company, while at other times it is dispersed across a number of companies which specialize in different markets. The choice between keeping companies separate or rolling them up into a giant

---

[4]Marc H. Meyer and Alvin P. Lehnerd, *The Power of Product Platforms*, The Free Press, New York, 1997.

monolith is best addressed with reference to tax, cultural, geographic, and management considerations. Private equity firms are examples of a product/company portfolio. When a private equity portfolio has dozens of companies, the bankruptcy of an individual company is less painful and costly.

Having a portfolio of products makes good strategic sense provided the portfolio is managed to "lead with cash". The key issues are these:

- How much cash is needed each year by each product for investment, marketing, and other product support requirements?
- How much cash will each product generate annually?
- What is the strategic importance of each product?
- Is there a process to identify products to keep and those to jettison?

The first two items in the list above are calculation-driven and are discussed later in this chapter. The third item requires a framework for analysis. One tool that has helped managers discriminate between products since the 1970s was developed by the Boston Consulting Group (BCG). Referred to as the growth-share matrix or the BCG matrix, the tool has simple data needs and provides an unambiguous message. I encourage its use because it forces companies to analytically compare their products/companies. The BCG matrix reviews a company's market share and its market growth. The presumption behind the matrix is that there exists a strong correlation between market share and profits and between market growth and investment needs. While the posited relationship between these concepts may not be universal, there is undoubtedly some degree of truth to them. Figure 6.3 illustrates the BCG matrix.

A high market share means that a company owns or controls a significant proportion of the market. High market growth means that sales of the product/service are rising rapidly. The BCG labeled products as stars when they have both high market share and high market growth. In the opposite corner of the matrix, dogs have low market share and low market growth. A product with high market share but low market growth is a cash cow. Finally, question marks are companies with low market share but high market growth. The

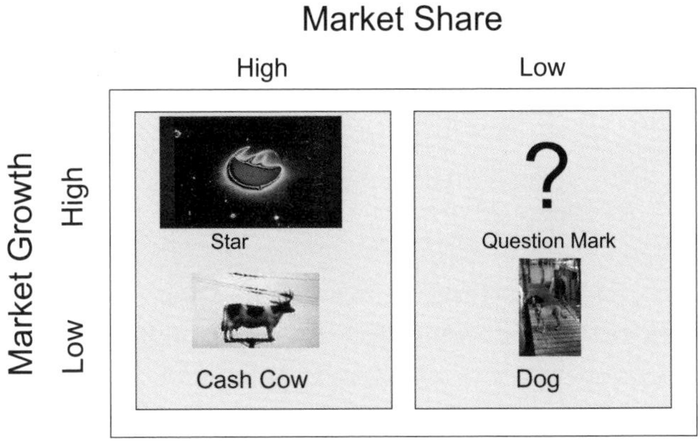

## Market Share

Fig. 6.3    The Boston Consulting Group Matrix.[5]

simple names create an easily remembered and highly symbolic tax-onomical classification.

Presumably stars are great companies: they are profitable play-ers in a growing market. Cash cows, too, are highly profitable but, unlike stars, they probably require little future investment. Dogs lack in both profits and future prospects. Finally, question marks are unimportant players in a growing market. A further generaliza-tion of the elements in the BCG matrix is that stars are often in newly emerging or technological markets, cash cows are in mature businesses, and question marks and dogs can be anywhere. Without strong turnaround skills, most companies want to dispose of their dogs. Buyers of dogs may be trying to consolidate a slow-growth industry, pursue an underutilized asset with a low-ball bid, or liqui-date the firm and sell off its assets.

Some analysts suggest that a good portfolio strategy combines products/companies in all parts of the BCG matrix excluding dogs. Their rationale is that a balanced portfolio creates a self-funding opportunity, with cows paying for stars and question marks. This view seems too simplistic to me. I would advocate having companies in all portions of the BCG matrix, even dogs, provided that their

---

[5]Source of copyright-free images: http://gimp-savvy.com/.

net cash flows justify their retention. Purchasing a dog for $1, when it has a net present value (NPV) that is greater than $1, is a good investment.

There are three possible goals for a portfolio of products/ companies. The first, as mentioned above, is to create balance. Balance extends beyond just investment needs (i.e., growth) to include riskiness, longevity (staying power), consumption of managerial time, and technological uncertainties. The second goal is alignment with the company's strategic framework. I am not talking here about core competencies and whether companies must stick with them; rather, the concern is to not let a product cause a company to abandon its strategic plan. It is better to reject a product than to slip away from a good strategy. The third goal is the most important: lead with cash. Products with negative discounted cash flow (DCF) but growing markets, or negative DCF but high market share, or both are bad products/companies that need to be dropped. There are few ways to ever rationalize maintaining a negative-DCF product, and I do not suggest that companies do so lightly.

## Setting Strategy with Cash

Let us imagine a company which has four products. To simplify the lesson, suppose that there is only one year in the future. For each product, the company should be able to determine its cash outflows (investments) and cash inflows. This situation is depicted in Fig. 6.4. The difference between the two figures is net cash flow or, in the case of a one-year example, the DCF.

Any product without positive net cash flow should be dropped. That is, any product, regardless of where it falls in the BCG matrix or how strategically it may fit, must earn positive cash flow for the firm; otherwise, it should be terminated. In Fig. 6.4, this situation corresponds with product 2, which has significant cash inflows but a larger cash outflow. In the case with just a single year, the analysis is simple and compelling. No one will argue with this interpretation when there is only a single year in the future. But in the real world, the problem is more complicated because the future contains many years and not just one.

## A World that Lasts a Single Year

| Cash Investment | | Cash Inflow | Net |
|---|---|---|---|
| $1,000,000 | Product 1 | $1,500,000 | $500,000 |
| $5,000,000 | Product 2 | $4,000,000 | ($1,000,000) |
| $9,000,000 | Product 3 | $10,000,000 | $1,000,000 |
| $21,000,000 | Product 4 | $27,000,000 | $6,000,000 |

Fig. 6.4   A Single-Year World and a Company with Four Products.

A common situation is that, over time, a product moves back and forth between positive and negative net cash flows. Figure 6.5 illustrates this point using a three-year time horizon for a single product. The DCF technique discussed in Chapter 5 is relied on to translate a multi-year view of cash flows into a single value, the DCF. This works whether the horizon includes 2 or 200 years. Then, all products/companies owned by a firm can be ranked according to their DCFs, as depicted in Fig. 6.6. Note that all products with negative

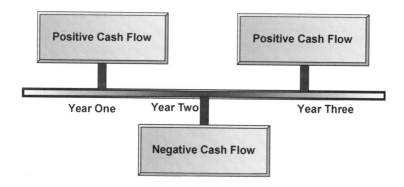

Fig. 6.5   A Single Product Over a Three-Year Time Horizon.

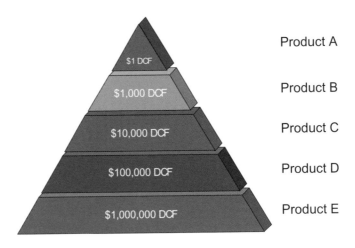

Fig. 6.6    Ranking of All Positive-DCF Products.

DCF have already been rejected from the figure. Now the question is how to decide which of the products in the figure to maintain.

If the firm has unlimited financial resources and will never encounter a budget constraint, it should continue all products with positive DCF. In Fig. 6.6, products A–E all have positive DCFs. While the firm would probably be reluctant to give up product E given its large expected DCF, a budget constraint might easily tip the scales against products A, B, and C based on their relatively low DCFs.

## Overview

Strategic choices guide a firm's product and company mix. Whether companies use Porter's five forces, employ the BCG matrix, or attempt to have a competitive advantage, the ultimate decision-making tool must be DCF. No product or company that does not yield a positive DCF can or should be maintained.

# 7. Change the Culture to One Based on Cash

Companies have cultures. Some cultures are beneficial; others are faulty. A faulty culture hinders a company's pursuit of its main goal. A beneficial culture brings together members of the company's team into a cohesive organization that works together to achieve the main goal. Cultures can be changed. Companies can transition from a harmful culture to one that is beneficial.

A culture is a set of values. Corporate values include concepts such as honesty, frugality, creativity, quality, etc. Let us consider a simple example of how a company has a set of values. As a youngster, perhaps you worked every Sunday morning helping your father in the backyard. His culture had unambiguous values: finish what you start, be a careful worker, and respect your tools. In addition to getting the yard cleaned up, he was probably trying to bequeath his values to you. Your experience in the backyard would have been worse if his culture had been, "Do it my way and don't ask any questions." With the latter culture, you would have hated working with him, probably would have done the job poorly, and today would probably employ somebody to cut your lawn. Culture, therefore, is incredibly important. The best workers with the best tools will be unsuccessful if the company's culture is flawed. A strong culture pulls a team together and motivates everyone to work hard.

Some companies are well known for their cultures. Google, for example, allows its workers to use a day a week to consider new ideas. Creativity is thus part of Google's culture. Southwest Airlines looks for people who work well in a team and bring humor to the workplace. Southwest wants to be known as the friendly airline. The point here is that companies establish their own culture, either by commission or omission. Deliberately creating a culture is better than letting a culture evolve on its own. By thoughtfully invoking values that benefit the company, a successful culture arises. Cultures that evolve on their own contain a mixture of both good and bad values.

My favorite example of how a culture evolves on its own is one I learned about when a student asked a CEO who was visiting my class what he was doing differently after a turnaround. He said, "I'm looking more closely at new sales opportunities." The man's wife had come to class with him and, when she heard his answer, she responded to a stunned classroom, "That's not right, John, you're playing a lot less golf." Before the turnaround, most days John had left work at noon to play golf. After he left, no one worked very hard and many others left work early too. The culture that John had created by his own behavior at the US$500 million enterprise which he had inherited is best described as "accepting of slackers and lethargy". Only after nearly failing and going through a bitter turnaround did John work to establish a more energetic culture that encouraged employees to work hard and be industrious.

Cultures are created, as the example above describes, by intentional and unintentional signals conveyed to the team. Workers respond to stimuli, whether or not they are intended to set the culture. The list of stimuli includes managerial actions, informal verbal or written communications, and formal regulations published in handbooks or other corporate disclosures. The first two are informal while the latter is formal. Informal clues are the best way to create a culture. When workers see their manager being diligent, they are motivated to do the same themselves. Likewise, when an employee is appropriately told that their behavior needs to change and they are told what modification to make, they are likely to change their behavior. In contrast, posting regulations or issuing proclamations is probably the least successful and most easily ignored way to try and change a culture. It is easy to walk past a posted sign or to delete an email, for example, but it is much harder to be nasty to customers when the boss is standing right next to you.

When creating or changing a corporate culture, the objective is not to neutralize or obliterate the individual, but rather to create a collective sense of community and common purpose. If this sounds like a platitude, it is probably because I am discussing it in the abstract. But be assured that a community with a common purpose and a realistic incentive system is a far more powerful tool than any single individual. Within the community, individual differences can and should exist. There is not a single acceptable behavior form. Diversity is permissible and acceptable. The only caveat is that the individual must conform to the basic fabric of the culture.

*Lead with Cash* encourages companies to remake their corporate cultures so that the achievement of cash flow becomes the central focus of all employees. It does not really matter what the current corporate culture is. What is important is that employees are deprogrammed away from their old ways of doing business and are enlightened to the advantages of having cash flow as the main goal. The basic idea is for employees to act as if they owned the company. Instead of being concerned about how to make their own job easier, they need to consider how to get their job done while at the same time increasing the company's cash flow.

Some cultural types commonly observed in companies are:

- The egocentric culture — I am the only one who matters. Only I should be praised and rewarded. Mistakes occur because of others.
- The 9-to-5 culture — This is only a job. What matters to me occurs outside the workplace.
- The OK culture — Do not make the job difficult. Agree to everything so that there is no unpleasantness at work, including contract terms, return policies, work rules, etc.
- The lord-of-the-manor culture — The boss is in charge. Never disagree or contradict the boss.

Each of these cultural types, if they exist at a company, should be altered since they inhibit the cash flow mentality. In none of them does the idea of maximizing cash flow appear anywhere on the agenda. For example, in an egocentric culture, individuals damage the cash flow efforts of others by blunting their good work. In the 9-to-5 culture, workers get their individual jobs done but never consider how the company's cash flow can be enhanced. In an OK culture, cash flow might be increased but only if it can be gained without creating a fuss. Finally, with the lord-of-the-manor culture, if the boss is not focused on cash flow, then neither is anyone else. None of these alternate cultures points the company's employees in the right direction.

The new culture should encourage the "lead with cash" mentality. By revising their mission, vision, and competency/core business statements to include the new focus on cash flow, companies communicate to all constituents that cash flow is the main goal and one which all units of the business are concentrated on. However, just making these changes is not enough. Doing lip service to the ideals of *Lead with Cash* but not following up with concrete actions may be even more harmful than doing nothing at all. If a company just speaks about cash flow but does nothing to force cash flow to the forefront, workers will return to the old way of doing business.

Several ideas that help to ensure the success of a cultural shift are:

- To have a leader in each group and unit who takes responsibility for implementing the changeover. Responsibility without power is risky. These leaders must be given the power to change everything: how business is conducted, who is doing it, what they are paid, etc.
- To have the organization frequently and consistently articulate the cash flow goal, both philosophically as well as in terms of a specific annual or quarterly target. Moreover, the company must continually update the entire staff on how closely the firm is tracking its cash flow goal.
- To publicly reward groups achieving their target and to penalize groups who block the cultural shift. Note that it is not advisable, at least in the short term, to punish groups which miss their target, since the difficulty in changing over from the old culture to the new differs between groups.

Care must be taken so that the cash flow goals of *Lead with Cash* are held not just by upper management and line managers, but also by those who work for them. Everyone in the organization must jump on board the new culture. Participation need not be overt or conspicuous, but it must affect how everyone conducts their daily activities. One idea is to have each team formally survey its members to inquire how they have changed their way of doing business as a result of changing the culture. The survey should also ask whether there is something which is inhibiting the worker from making a change. These surveys should be confidential, since it is likely that holdovers from the old culture, especially those nearing retirement or fearful of not having a place in the new organization, may consciously or unconsciously work to subvert the implantation of the new culture. A final question to ask is whether there are adequate incentives in place to encourage the transition. Just keeping a job may be incentive enough for some, but for others who were highly rewarded in some fashion by the old culture, the incentive system must be accommodative to their situation.

A company with a strong culture has teams of workers who feel perfectly aligned with the organization's goals and values. Incentive systems are an important part of this alignment, but so too is the way in which employees sense that the new culture is in fact the best one for the firm. To encourage this, companies should have all employees participate in educational forums that explain the purpose and benefits of the "lead with cash" culture. After some time, these forums should be conducted by teams that have made changes which effectively improved the company's cash flow. Documenting and disseminating success stories leads to further success, as other teams imitate the actions of the successful group or as they try to outdo the other team's success.

Successful companies are the least likely to immediately jump onto the "lead with cash" bandwagon. Instead, most new adherents will be companies that are anticipating, currently facing, or recovering from financial distress. In some respects, this is actually fortunate since troubled companies and their employees are the most accepting of change. When people fear for their jobs and their financial security, and when someone presents them with a new idea that has been demonstrated to provide companies with greater cash flow, financial security, and long-term growth prospects, they are more likely to try it out. This suggests that, when presenting the new cultural imperative, examples of other companies should be provided that showcase how they were in a similar situation to the troubled firm and how, after changing their culture, they overcame difficulties and prospered.

To assist in this mission, I have asked several of the best turnaround and crisis managers in the world to discuss examples of companies they have worked with that have modified their behavior and become better companies. These vignettes appear in Chapter 16 of this book. Each of the turnaround and crisis managers is well known, highly skilled, and widely respected. Managers implementing the new "lead with cash" culture should read these examples and be prepared to summarize them when they discuss the changes with their teams.

# 8. Designing Cash Flow into Systems

No matter how much a company and its employees want to put the "lead with cash" system to work, their objective will not be met fully (if at all) unless the company redesigns its systems and procedures to accommodate the method. Existing corporate structures, incentive systems, and reporting mechanisms are inadequate for the task of making cash flow the central objective of the entire company. In order to make the transition from the old way of doing business to the "lead with cash" method, organizations need to be redesigned so that cash flow becomes an essential concern at every stage of business.

This task sounds overwhelming (if not impossible) to those just learning about the "lead with cash" discipline since they know that business today, except for in specialized parts of the organization such as the financial function, is not controlled with cash flow as an objective. It is not just that cash flow is not an objective; cash flow is not even considered when decisions are made throughout most of the organization. This problem can be overcome. What is required is (1) a redesign of how and what information flows throughout the organization, (2) greater awareness of what other parts of the organization need, and (3) knowledge of what actions are taken and by whom when targets are not met. The key is to design corporate systems so that cash flow is constantly at the center of every decision.

Refashioning businesses to focus on cash flow is far less complicated than sending a person to the moon or building a newly designed jetliner with synthetic materials, new specifications, and new operating characteristics. How do such out-of-the-ordinary things get accomplished? In some cases, the answer is "systems engineering". Systems engineering is a field of study that has emerged in recent years to help organizations achieve complex tasks. The same principles that helped send a man to the moon can be applied to help companies systematize and refashion themselves to align all of their parts so that they are focused on the main goal of cash flow. In this chapter, I show how systems engineering methods and other techniques can help any company change itself to facilitate the implementation of a "lead with cash" program.

The science of systems engineering is a useful tool to help implement a "lead with cash" system. When systems engineering evolved nearly 75 years ago, society engaged in few complex projects. Today, complex undertakings are far more common — ranging from the design of computer software and the launch of spaceships to the management of critical patient care in hospitals — and systems engineering techniques are often found abetting those efforts.

What does systems engineering do? Perhaps the most important contribution of systems engineering is how it trains project participants to focus on the corporation's overall mission while at the same time performing their own tasks. Normally, employees "can't see the forest for the trees." It is not that they are terrible workers, but rather that they are isolated workers who are doing their job to the best of their ability. The problem is that they are doing their job, but are not extending themselves in order to consider what the company needs. It is not unusual in complex organizations for employees to only perceive themselves and their own tasks; obviously they are aware of others, but they do not examine what makes those other parts of the business work, how they relate to their own section, and what can be done to coordinate between departments so as to accomplish the goals of the company.

For example, consider the conflict at a hospital between employees whose job is to worry about controlling costs and other employees whose task is to help patients get well. The first group of employees may question why certain diagnostic tests are performed and why a patient has been put into a single room at the hospital. The other group responds that the tests are essential diagnostic tools and that the patient has an infectious disease and should not be in a double room. To some extent, these two sets of goals are permanently incompatible, yet they are both mission-critical. That is, they both need to be performed despite their incompatibility.

I believe that this incompatibility is not essential, but is a result of the current system controlling how companies are managed. In a "lead with cash" model, the two hospital groups learn to better understand the goals and objectives of the other group and how to be more accommodating to those needs. Notice I did not say how to acquiesce to the other group's needs, nor did I say how to manipulate the other group to accommodate one's own needs. The best outcome is when the two groups learn to communicate between themselves and work together to achieve what is in the company's (i.e., the hospital's) best interest. The number cruncher allows more diagnostic tests after learning that a quicker diagnosis results in earlier treatment and patient release. Medical personnel stop ordering duplicative tests after learning how those actions negatively affect the hospital's cash flow, since insurance companies are not paying for duplicative tests.

Fragmentation, rivalry, and hostility, like that described in the hospital example, are not uncommon amongst business departments. Some companies fight these tendencies by creating process-oriented businesses that flatten management structures. In a flat business model, employees are not assigned to a specific task and instructed to remain in their silo forever. Instead, everyone works on a single task contributing what they can and helping others. However, a flat business model probably would not help in the hospital example above, since the task of the medical doctor cannot be shared with other departments. Moreover, process-oriented organizations are a good systems engineering solution, but *not* for the problem that *Lead with Cash* is trying to solve. Flat business models do not increase the average employee's recognition of the fact that cash flow is the central focus of the company. A different solution is required to achieve that goal.

The cash flow problem for most businesses comes in two forms. First, while employees do their job, they do not think about how what they are doing affects cash flow. These workers are not trying to impair cash flow; rather, they are either (1) unaware of cash flow or (2) do not understand why they should worry about cash flow, seeing it as "someone else's job". Second, as employees perform their own tasks, they reduce the cash flow contribution from other sections/ groups within the organization either intentionally or inadvertently. Sometimes employees are unaware that their actions produce a cash flow effect elsewhere in the organization, and at other times they do not understand why they should care if a different group in the organization produces less cash flow than it might otherwise or does not produce any cash flow at all.

Basically, employees fail to achieve what the "lead with cash" model teaches either because of a lapse in their knowledge or because they do not understand the interrelationships between departments. Both problems are correctable. The first is resolved through adequate training aimed at teaching the fundamentals of cash flow to all employees. The second is more difficult to address, but the rewards from doing so are greater.

Cross-departmental cash flow issues, such as those in the hospital example above, are found throughout companies virtually everywhere that two departments intersect. Just consider these few examples. The sales department is trying to increase revenues by selling more goods, but is told by the production department that output cannot be increased because production cannot buy any more raw materials inventory due to a budget constraint. Or, the IT department wants to hire an outside consultant to manage the upgrading of a computer system, but the human resources department objects since several existing employees purportedly can accomplish the switchover themselves. In both examples, cash flow can be increased if the two groups work through their differences. Systems engineering is a tool that helps organizations resolve these internal disputes.

In its simplest form, systems engineering does three things:

(1) It ensures that all groups and individuals hear and understand what the main goal of the organization is. The main goal is articulated and refined by management.

(2) It arranges a fact sheet detailing the operating goals of each unit in the organization, and identifies how the goals of one part of the company can interfere with the goals of another part. It proposes mechanisms to allow cooperation between groups so as to foster the enhancement of the main goal while acknowledging that each unit's own objectives must be met, provided that they do not interfere with the main goal.

(3) It establishes a continuous review system to monitor how well the new guidelines move the enterprise toward the achievement of the main goal.

Companies need to redesign their systems so that recognition of cash flow is a persistent presence whenever a decision is made. The key to a successful redesign of a company's system is the way it balances the goals of individual units against the company's main goal.

Let us start by thinking about redesigning something simpler than a company's business units. For example, imagine there is a small mountain town that has a reservoir filled with water. One potential use of that water would be to sell it to the ski mountain in town so that they could make artificial snow. A second use would be to sell it to the local electric utility, which would use it to power their hydro-electric facility. Suppose the utility offers a price that is twice that offered by the mountain. Simple arithmetic would argue for accepting the utility's offer. But a deeper analysis finds that, without artificial snow, tourists do not come to town, jobs are lost, and ironically the utility would need to generate less electricity. If we suppose that the town's main goal is for all residents to have jobs, then the option of selling all the water to the utility is inferior to the option of selling some water to the utility to allow it to make the electricity needed in the town and selling the remaining water to the ski mountain to make snow and bring skiers into town. This outcome satisfies (not maximizes) both the main goal and the secondary goal, making it the superior choice.

Decision making before the redesign takes place involves a simple calculation of which choice produces the most money. After the redesign, the decision-making process involves a larger frame of reference, involving both a main goal and individual group goals. To use a word from psychology, decision making becomes concerned with the "Gestalt". Gestalt in psychology assumes that the whole organism is more important than all the individual parts. Applying the Gestalt philosophy to the redesign of a company's processes means that the needs of the company are given greater weight than the needs of any constituent part. That is, the main goal is recognized as having primacy over individual goals. The Gestalt philosophy is willing to suspend a secondary goal for a brief time and to permanently subordinate it in favor of achieving the main goal.

In redesigning a company's systems, the same principles apply. Let us start by identifying four essential parts of an idealized business, as seen in Fig. 8.1, to give a sense of the breadth of issues involved.[1] Obviously, hundreds of critical tasks/functions are not included in the figure; this is for simplicity purposes only. In practice, any number of business components can be modified following the program laid out below.

Figure 8.1 suggests that a business does four things. Thinking of these four functions linearly, the company starts by hiring workers and buying supplies and then producing a product/service and selling it. Nothing is new or unusual here; I have just pared the thousands of processes that a business conducts down to four essential

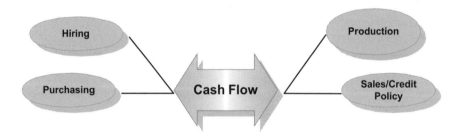

Fig. 8.1    A Systems View of a Company.

---

[1]Limiting ourselves to just four components keeps the analysis simple while at the same time providing enough complexity to make the analysis relevant.

functions. In the middle of the figure sits the main goal of all this activity: cash flow. The figure does not reveal the secondary objectives of the managers and employees who conduct the four individual tasks. That is, the figure does not show the objectives driving the teams that hire workers, etc. It is probably fair to say, however, that they are focused on concerns other than cash flow.

Table 8.1 provides some insight into the four individual groups and speculates on what their group objectives might be. These are unit-specific goals and are not necessarily (and probably not) concerned with the company's main goal. Each group in the table is shown to have two goals (labeled 1 and 2), though in reality they may have many different goals. Goal 1 is assumed to be the group's first or foremost concern, while goal 2 is the group's less important, but still relevant, secondary goal.

Businesses not working under the "lead with cash" mantra are likely to hold meetings with senior-level executives and group heads that would conclude with modification and then approval for the individual goals of the four groups listed in Table 8.1. After receiving approval from the executive team, each group operates relatively independently, provided that it achieves its stated goals. Companies in the "lead with cash" mold, however, operate differently.

Table 8.1  Goals of the Four Units of a Typical Business.

| Group/ Team | Group Goal 1 | Group Goal 2 |
|---|---|---|
| Hiring | Hire the number of workers requested by the other groups. | Minimize hiring costs and future compensation of hired workers. |
| Purchasing | Purchase sufficient materials to meet the needs of production. | Minimize the costs of items purchased. |
| Production | Produce the number of units requested by the sales department. | Minimize the costs of producing these goods. |
| Sales | Sell all the goods produced. | Maximize the revenues earned from the sales of goods. |

PART A
Conventional Companies

PART B
"Lead with Cash" Companies

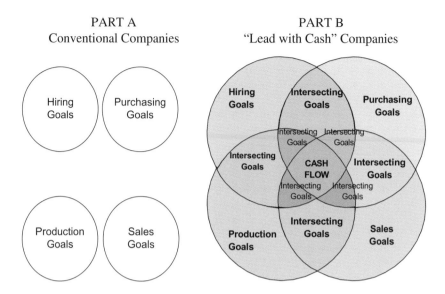

Fig. 8.2    Comparing "Lead with Cash" and Normal Companies.

Figure 8.2 shows how the four groups operate in a conventional company and in a company following the "lead with cash" dictum. The conventional firm's four groups submit unit goals and, once approval is obtained, operate semi-autonomously. In contrast, the "lead with cash" firm understands that there are important intersecting goals linking the four groups and that they should not operate independently. Figure 8.2 shows the following intersections between group goals:

- Major intersecting goals directly connecting any two of the groups;
- Additional intersecting goals that combine three groups at one time; and
- A final intersecting goal that combines all four groups in terms of maximizing cash flow.

Probably the most important contribution of the "lead with cash" model is in the recognition of the linkages between groups. It is not enough to say that firms should focus on cash. That is just a platitude along the lines of, "I hope my political party wins." To effectively help a political party win, a person needs to devote money and time. Likewise, saying "let's focus the company on cash" is not enough; what is needed is the identification of linkages between groups in the organization and how those linkages can affect cash flows.

Returning to the example depicted in Fig. 8.2, the four groups have major intersections between themselves and the other three groups, plus minor intersections between themselves and several of the other groups at the same time. Thinking about the major intersections involving just the hiring group, that group's goals have unambiguous intersections with those of the purchasing, production, and sales groups.[2] Table 8.2 reproduces Table 8.1, but adds a column showing a possible major intersection between the groups. In the table, it is assumed that the hiring group hits its two goals: it hires the requisite number of workers and it minimizes the cost of those workers. The group minimizes its costs by hiring less experienced, lower-quality workers. In other words, the group has performed its function very well by meeting both of its approved unit goals. This sort of outcome occurs frequently among companies managed as in Part A of Fig. 8.2 because of the lack of consideration given to how group goals intersect.

Table 8.2's column on the far right-hand side identifies the consequences of the hiring group meeting its goals without concern for how its decisions affect the other groups. Low-quality workers are less productive. Purchasing and production fall behind their number one goals as a consequence of the hiring group hiring low-quality workers. Lower-quality workers are more wasteful with supplies, and the firm soon discovers that it is understocked with raw materials and other inventory. Similarly, production cannot meet its goals because there are too few supplies and because workers are less productive. Sales also runs into difficulties. Not only can the sales target (goal 1) not be met if too few goods are produced (this is an example of a joint intersection involving purchasing [not enough supplies], production [not enough production], and sales), but goal 2 is not met if

---

[2]Hiring is used as an example only. The discussion could similarly begin with any of the four groups.

Table 8.2    Extended Goals of the Four Units of a Typical Business.

| Group/ Team | Group Goal 1 | Group Goal 2 | Major Intersection with the Hiring Group |
|---|---|---|---|
| Hiring | Hire the number of workers requested by the other groups. | Minimize hiring costs and future compensation of hired workers. | |
| Purchasing | Purchase sufficient materials to meet the needs of production. | Minimize the costs of items purchased. | Will need more supplies if low-productivity workers are hired. |
| Production | Produce the number of units requested by the sales department. | Minimize the costs of producing these goods. | Will not be able to hit the production target if low-productivity workers are hired. |
| Sales | Sell all the goods produced. | Maximize the revenues earned from the sales of goods. | Low-productivity workers may reduce quality and affect sales. |

customers return many of the goods purchased due to their being of lower quality than expected.

Although complicated to describe, multi-group intersections and associated negative consequences are not infrequent occurrences. For example, if purchasing signs purchase orders with less reliable and less expensive foreign suppliers, there is a good chance that the materials will arrive late or not at all. In that case, production and sales both suffer. Since the four operations conducted by our fictitious company are performed serially, with hiring coming first and sales occurring last, multi-group interactions are more common with the earliest actions and less common with the later events.

How do companies move from Part A in Fig. 8.2 to Part B? That is, how do they inculcate their groups to recognize that the main goal, maximizing cash flow, is impeded and harmed by the failure of each group to account for how its actions influence the other groups in the organization? The trick is to devise a series of strategies, tactics, and methods that focus the entire organization on (1) achieving the main goal and (2) creating an awareness of how each group's actions affect the ability of the other groups to achieve their individual goals.

One device that helps get everyone to see the big picture, the Gestalt, is a decision matrix. A decision matrix highlights gains and losses to the company from deviations from each group's unit goals. In other words, the matrix reveals the costs (in terms of cash flow) of hiring low-quality workers to the purchasing, production, and sales departments. The matrix might show that, for every dollar saved by hiring lower-quality workers, $2 is lost due to purchasing difficulties, $1 is lost due to production problems, and $4 is lost due to sales issues. The $1 in savings then actually costs the firm $7, or $6 net of the savings. Without the decision matrix, many people probably know about the negative consequences of hiring poor-quality workers, yet they need the quantification that the matrix provides in order to put their concerns into action. With this information identified, the hiring team rethinks its plan, returns to management, and submits new group goals. Its added goal might be that workers will have sufficient talent to meet the needs of the company. Adding that goal is a "lead with cash" action. The firm's goals become dynamic rather than remaining static. Each group looks out for the needs of the other groups. That way, the main goal is achieved and everyone participates in its achievement.

Following a move to get a company's groups to work together, the next step is to realign the corporation's incentive system to facilitate collaborative behavior. Conventional incentive schemes fail to create a proper alignment between the various parts of an organization; my rewards are not linked to your performance. Let us use baseball as a starting point. Suppose a team hires a superstar player. He is given a contract worth millions of dollars, which includes a bonus for every home run he hits in the coming year. Being a rational human being, the player will take every opportunity to hit for the fences when he is at bat. While fans might appreciate the thrill when the player connects and hits one out of the park, the manager will probably be pulling out his or her hair when the player strikes out with a man in scoring position in the ninth inning. If the player's bonus had combined the home run goal with a team-oriented goal of winning games, the player might have tried to get the run in from third base rather than trying to hit a home run.

The strategy for fixing an incentive system is actually very simple. Bonuses and other rewards should be allocated based on (1) the performance of the company; (2) the accomplishment of individual goals; and (3) most importantly, the success of areas in the company whose goals are interrelated with the specific unit in question. In other words, the incentive system needs to account for the interactions between group goals. Part B in Fig. 8.2 shows a series of interconnected circles. The incentive system needs to mirror that depiction with rewards given out for the achievement of not just a group's unit goals, but also the goals that interrelate with that group's goals. Caution is necessary, though, to ensure that the reward system is not too complicated. Companies will find that an extra part of complexity in the reward system, after accounting for the major interrelationships, will add very little to improved performance.

Every company and every unit will have its own special mix of these three important components: company, group, and interrelationships. For example, in one case, a group's incentive scheme might be tied equally to the three components. If the company achieves a specified level of cash flow, if the group hits its own target, and if the other groups whose success depends in part on what this group does also achieve their targets, then this group gets its full bonus. The formula would specify by how much the bonuses would be reduced should any of the three components not be achieved. In another case, a group with only limited control over things which affect other groups might have its reward system structured as 45-percent company, 45-percent group, and 10-percent interrelationships.

The final step in devising systems to accommodate cash flow is to modify the reporting mechanism so that the proper signals are being sent and received. If groups are unaware that related groups are failing to meet their targets, then they have no reason to change their own behavior. Information not only informs, but also leads to action.

Obviously, cash flow must be reported; so too should intermediate goals. Using the example above, the production team's actual output should be reported and compared against its goal; similarly, the sales department's number of returns due to low quality should be reported and balanced against previous performance. In other words, information should be provided that helps groups to (1) encourage other groups to modify their behavior to help them meet their targets, and (2) limit the ability of poorly performing groups to hide their inadequate performance or their lack of cooperation.

Managers need to meet with each group and determine what each group needs from the other groups. Based on this knowledge, it should be possible to assemble a list of information that needs to be communicated amongst various groups.

# 9. Creating Cash with Optimal Pricing Decisions

The easiest thing to do is to change prices. The hardest thing to do is to change prices. This statement of opposites, in the style of Charles Dickens' *A Tale of Two Cities*, has a simple meaning: any fool can change a price, but only a wise man can do it well. This cautionary statement is not intended to dissuade companies from creating cash flow by utilizing the tactic of price changes. Rather, its purpose is to warn companies to know in advance what they are doing before they make an irreversible mistake. The unintended consequence of changing a price may be lower revenues and profits than before prices were changed. To avoid bringing cost structure and returns to scale into the analysis in this chapter (this is not the correct forum), pricing decisions are discussed in the context of revenues alone. Naturally, profits are what really matter and not revenues, so the reader should ask themselves what their firm's cost structure is like and how it responds to either increases or decreases in unit sales. Specifically, they need to know whether costs change in step with output changes or whether output economies lead to cost savings (losses) as output rises (falls).

Price changes are probably the best cash flow-generating tool in a company's arsenal. They work immediately and, if things go according to plan, they result in rapidly accelerating cash flow. The success of price changes in raising cash flow depends on the consumers' response to the new price level. Consumers respond to price changes over both the short term and the long term. The short-term response may be mild with only a minor reduction in sales, but the longer-term response may be far more dramatic. The limited short-term response may confuse the pricing manager and incorrectly signal that further price changes are in order. For example, when gasoline prices increase, consumers continue to use their older, inefficient vehicle for some time; eventually, however, they buy a new, more efficient vehicle and reduce their gasoline consumption.

What separates good and bad pricing tactics is whether companies understand and exploit their customers' demand elasticity. The simple elasticity rule is that revenues rise when prices are *increased* if demand is inelastic, but revenues increase when prices are *decreased* if demand is elastic. The word "elastic" describes the responsiveness of unit sales to price changes. An elastic demand is one which changes dramatically when prices change; an inelastic demand changes far less in response to a price change. What sets changes in unit sales apart is whether the response equals, exceeds, or is less than the percentage change in price. For example, a 10-percent change in prices that leads to a 5-percent drop in demand is called inelastic because demand responds by less than the price change. In contrast, a 10-percent price decrease that leads to a 17-percent increase in demand is an elastic response.

Knowing product elasticity is not enough to ensure that price changes are applied correctly. In addition to price elasticity, companies need to know about their customers' incomes, demographics (urban/rural, north/south, family size, marital status, etc.), employment history, and so on. Prices should not be changed without a full understanding of how customers, competitors, and regulators will react to them.

Elasticity summarizes a multitude of forces that influence how the consumer responds to a price change. Included among these forces are:

- The number of competitors in the market;
- The price level of competing goods;
- The frequency with which the product is repurchased;
- The perceived quality of your product relative to your competitors;

- The importance of the purchase in the consumer's total spending; and
- Product tie-ins that create selling opportunities.

Each of these is discussed below.

## The Number of Competitors in the Market

Companies that face fewer competitors have more ability to raise prices, all other things being the same. The ability to raise prices is called pricing power. Competition is a powerful force requiring as few as a single hostile competitor to keep a company from being able to sustain a price increase. The other force affecting how easily a company can raise price is customer loyalty. The more loyal a company's customers are, the greater the firm's ability to raise price.

The graph in Fig. 9.1 illustrates the best and worst cases for the number of competitors and customer loyalty. Companies with few competitors and loyal customers like Apple Inc. have historically charged their consumers more than the competition. Apple arguably has no competitors, though there are reasonably close substitutes for

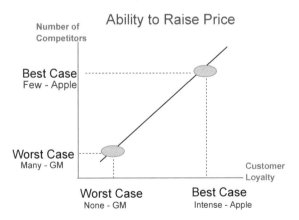

Fig. 9.1   Ability to Raise Price: The Interaction of Number of Competitors and Customer Loyalty.

its products. Moreover, Apple's customers feel that the unique characteristics of its products are desirable. When its number of competitors and customer loyalty are put together, Apple has tremendous pricing power.

In the opposite corner, General Motors (GM) found itself with numerous competitors, both domestic and foreign, and a fleet of vehicles that consumers viewed as inferior. Before its restructuring in 2009, GM had no pricing power. In fact, the only way that GM could sell most of its products was by underpricing the competition. A similar-sized Toyota was priced about 10–15 percent higher than the corresponding GM vehicle.

## The Price Level of Competing Goods

The prices of some goods are noticeably low relative to their competitors' prices. For example, in some U.S. states Trader Joe's sells its Charles Shaw brand of wine for US$1.99 a bottle. The wine is of good quality and is probably equal to a US$10.00 bottle from other providers. This price disparity gives Trader Joe's a great deal of pricing power. It could probably raise the price of its wine somewhat and not lose many customers. Of course, Trader Joe's uses the wine to attract customers and raising the price might be counterproductive to that objective. Having competitors who charge higher prices creates pricing power for the firm with lower prices.

## The Frequency with Which the Product Is Repurchased

Some products are purchased daily; others are purchased infrequently; some are purchased only once in a lifetime. Products with regular purchase schedules, like milk or newspapers, afford the consumer the opportunity to compare providers and find less costly offerings. This reduces pricing power. In contrast, products that are rarely purchased, like coffins or houses, produce less informed consumers.

Pricing power rises with consumer ignorance (infrequent purchases) and the provider earns incremental return as a result.

## The Perceived Quality of Your Product Relative to Your Competitors

Consumers mentally create a ranking of companies, identifying some as having high-quality products and others as being inferior providers. The actual difference between similar products may in fact be slight, but consumers may nonetheless be willing to pay a substantial premium to the provider perceived as being of high quality. For example, Verizon Communications Inc.'s wireless network is perceived by many consumers as being the best, and not surprisingly Verizon's rate plans command a premium price. Perceived quality creates pricing power.

## The Importance of the Purchase in the Consumer's Total Spending

A can of soda is cheap whilst lobster is expensive. When the corner store raises the price of soda by 10 percent, the consumer hardly notices the extra few cents. But when an expensive restaurant raises the price of a lobster dinner by 10 percent, some of its consumers may react by ordering less expensive fare. Selling a product whose price is a small percentage of the consumer's total budget (e.g., printer paper to a company may qualify as an example of a low-cost item) creates pricing power for the producer.

## Product Tie-ins That Create Selling Opportunities

Tie-in sales can vastly increase a company's profitability. This prospect arises in part because the consumer is focused on understanding and pricing the main product and is less attuned to the market for tie-ins. It also occurs because the tie-in sale is generally less expensive (see the section above on the importance of the purchase in the consumer's total spending). Good managers seek out tie-in sales opportunities.

Examples of tie-in sales include purchasers of computers, automobiles, and other expensive products who worry about the reliability of their purchase. Vendors of these products take advantage of these fears to offer extended warranty or service contracts that are often never utilized. For example, companies that buy expensive enterprise software realize that they have tied the entire firm's future to the success of the software. Fear that once the software is installed the system will stop working leads these purchasers to buy extended service contracts. Buyers make substantial monthly payments to manufacturers for continued service and care. In this example, fear gives the seller pricing power on its tie-in product. The seller may even be willing to price the basic product at or near its cost if they can earn their profit by selling a tie-in service contract. Profit margins on service contracts usually exceed those on manufactured goods. For that reason, International Business Machine Corporation (IBM) has transitioned its business towards services.

## Pricing Strategies

Companies with pricing power generally have products with inelastic demand. It is hard to raise prices when demand is elastic, as a price increase would drive away customers. Cash flow is created by raising prices on inelastically demanded products.

Sound pricing strategies also include lowering prices. In June 2009, Apple introduced the 3GS version of its iPhone at US$199 and US$299, depending on memory, in order to compete with new offerings from its competitors. Apple then reinvigorated its older 3G model by cutting its price from US$199 to just US$99. Price cuts are especially useful when demand is elastic. In that case, the lower price attracts more than enough new consumers whose incremental revenues replace the revenues lost from existing consumers via the price cut. The fear in price cutting is that consumers will change their product perception. After a price cut, consumers may think of the product as (1) inferior in quality to its competitors or (2) a marketplace loser unless the competitor's product is also cut in price. Procter & Gamble Co. (P&G) wrestled with this conundrum during the recession of 2009. Reduced consumer incomes made a dent in P&G's sales and reduced its profits. To combat this loss, P&G introduced lower-priced products throughout its product categories. Similarly, Williams-Sonoma, Inc. suffered a surprising loss after trying to hold the line on product price when sales declined by 22 percent in the first quarter of 2009. The company subsequently introduced lower-priced goods and also reduced the prices it charged on goods already stocked.

## Using Pricing to Create Cash Flow

It is hard to categorically state when a company should raise prices since every product is different. However, I like to think that, in addition to knowing and understanding a product's demand elasticity, the five simple rules listed below are a good guide to making decisions on pricing:

(1) Consider what the consumer is willing to pay.
(2) Understand the value of your product.
(3) Consider the product life cycle.
(4) Utilize segment pricing.
(5) Do not change prices too often.

Each of these is discussed in turn.

### Consider What the Consumer Is Willing to Pay

No matter how good a coffee maker your company sells, few consumers are going to be willing to pay more than $50 for one. Of course, there are coffee aficionados who would pay $1,000 or more for a perfect espresso maker, but it is doubtful that there are enough of them to support a general rise in coffee maker prices. Home-brewed coffee is a real money saver versus buying coffee at the local coffee shop, but when it comes to buying a home coffee maker most consumers are quite satisfied with a dependable $50 product. Makers of coffee machines may be doing poorly financially and hoping to take advantage of a recession to attract consumers away from coffee shops, but they are strongly advised to consider how much their consumers are willing to pay before they raise prices.

On the other hand, precise information on what consumers will pay is generally lacking. For that reason, companies need to be careful in saying "no one would ever pay that much for our popcorn". For example, in 1976, Orville Redenbacher got American consumers to accept higher-priced popcorn by telling them that his popcorn was better. This culinary matter is subject to debate, but it is undoubtedly true that Orville Redenbacher popcorn sells for a multiple of the prices charged by other brands and for generic popcorn.

It is easy to think that consumers will accept a higher-priced product without adequate evidence to support that claim. Making price changes without information often leads to mistakes. In 2009, the New York Yankees built a new stadium. Some Yankee executives decided that consumers would pay up to US$2,500 for front-row box seats. They were wrong. After just a few weeks with many empty seats, the Yankees announced a price decrease of up to 50 percent. On the other hand, the Yankees are getting up to US$1,250 for seats that had been selling for less than US$250 before the new stadium was built.

## Understand the Value of Your Product

Sometimes companies confuse the cost of making something with its value to consumers. As a consequence, they misprice their product. This lesson has been learned well by companies like Sony, Swatch, and Nissan, who make extensive use of product platforms. Product platforms reduce the differential between the costs of making several products; what they do not affect is how the consumer views or values the different products. For example, Volkswagen Group's 7L product platform is at the core of various large sport utility vehicle (SUV) models, including the Audi Q7, the Porsche Cayenne, and the

VW Touareg. Yet, in 2009 the list prices of the various models were US$43,500 for the Audi, US$45,000 for the Porsche, and US$39,300 for the VW. Undoubtedly the cars are not the same, but they are very similar. Why does the Porsche cost so much more? One answer is that consumers value Porsches more than they value VWs or Audis. Value is not necessarily related to cost.

Companies that underestimate the value of their product may underprice it if they base product pricing on the cost of production. Consumers of these products are generally very happy and see the product as great value. On the other hand, when companies overestimate the value of their product, they price the product too high and face consumer resistance. One way to monitor the price–value relationship is to compare your product and its price to those of *all* your competitors. Look for imbalances in either the price or the value spectrum; then, decide if that has occurred by choice or by chance. Companies that allow the marketplace to position their product pricing rather than doing it themselves are likely to face either profit shortfalls or excess inventory.

### Consider the Product Life Cycle

As a product ages, its value generally declines. In general, the best opportunity for a high price is when the product is introduced. Companies can manage this price attrition by regularly introducing new products to coincide with the decline in the price point for existing products.[1] Figure 9.2 illustrates this notion.

The introduction of new products must be staged to (1) avoid confusing consumers who might wait to buy if they anticipate that another new product is on the way, and (2) allow maximal sales of each product at the high introductory price. Waiting too long, though, creates opportunities for competitors to enter the market and risks making the company look stale.

---

[1]New products need to include components that increase their value over existing products.

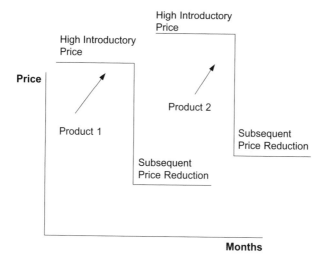

Fig. 9.2  Introducing Products to Manage Product Life Cycles.

## *Utilize Segment Pricing*

Marriott International has a hotel for every price point, from JW Marriott Hotels & Resorts at the high end to Fairfield Inn hotels at the low end. The key to segment pricing is to determine the price–quality relationship that maximizes cash flow. Figure 9.3 contains data on a firm with three products that essentially fill the same consumer needs. The products range from high to medium to low quality. The issues facing the company are: how high can the high-quality product be priced, how low should the low-quality product be priced, and where in the middle should the medium-quality product be priced? The example in the figure presents a nonlinear price–quality relationship. That is, the medium-quality product is priced closer to the high-quality product than to the low-quality product. The only way for the firm to discover the price–quality relationship that maximizes its cash flow is by trial and error. The thing to avoid in this process is confusing or upsetting the consumer. A large enough company should be able to conduct these trials in a confined space and thereby cause the least disruption and risk to the company's cash flow.

Fig. 9.3   Price–Quality Relationship in Segment Pricing.

## Do Not Change Prices Too Often

Having just told companies to experiment with their prices to discover the best price–quality relationship, this final point urges companies to avoid developing a reputation as a frequent price changer. Companies with such a reputation are viewed as deceitful or worse. Moreover, consumers are easily discombobulated when they find that a product has a different price today than it had yesterday. This does not occur the first time a company changes its price, but with a sufficient number of price changes even the most sanguine consumer becomes rattled.

# 10. Rethinking Capital Budgeting

In Chapter 5, discounted cash flow (DCF) and net present value (NPV) were introduced as important decision-making tools. Amongst the many critical business applications of DCF and NPV analysis is capital budgeting. Capital budgeting analyzes long-term investments such as machines, plants, or products in a framework which enables decision makers to quantify the financial worth of an investment. A key attribute of capital budgeting is that it creates a cardinal ranking that facilitates comparison between alternate investments. This chapter introduces another capital budgeting decision-making tool, payback period, and a hybrid version of it, discounted payback, as an alternative or supplemental methodology. The advantage of payback analysis versus NPV analysis is how it focuses on the timing of cash and cash flows.

The important contribution of DCF and internal rate of return (IRR)[1] is that they condense a large volume of time-related cost and profit data into a single parameter which is compared across projects and is used as a basis for decision making. A simple example helps to

---

[1] In his book, *The Theory of Interest* (Macmillan, London, 1930), Irving Fisher discussed the concept of the rate at which an investment has a return greater than its costs. This is what I mean by NPV. John Keynes, in his book, *The General Theory of Employment Interest and Money* (Palgrave Macmillan, Basingstoke, UK, 1936), wrote about the marginal efficiency of capital (MEC), which is the interest rate that converts the NPV to a zero value. MEC is now called the internal rate of return, or IRR.

explain this point. Let us start with a firm that is considering an investment which will have a payoff over many future years, as depicted in Table 10.1. The table reports that the investment costs the firm $100.00 at the end of the first year and that it provides the firm with $25.00 profit at the end of each of the next six years. The recurring question from decision makers is whether an investment is worthwhile. Prior to Fisher and Keynes introducing NPV[2] and IRR, respectively, a number of rudimentary tools were employed to decide the answer to this question.[3] The most basic analytical tool compares the project's total profits against its total cost. Since $150.00 (total profits) is greater than $100.00 (total costs), the project passes the simplest test.

What makes the simple answer unacceptable is the fact that the profit is earned over a six-year time period. Everyone knows that a dollar in hand today is worth more than a dollar received tomorrow. This fact is referred to as the time value of money. The time value of money is without a doubt one of the key innovations of modern finance. Irving Fisher, in his 1930 book, *The Theory of Interest*, said that a firm has a cost of capital[4] and that future profits should be

Table 10.1 Jones and Morrison Plush Toy Company — Capital Budgeting Calculation.

| Year | Costs | Profits |
|------|-------|---------|
| 1 | $100.00 | $ 0.00 |
| 2 | $ 0.00 | $25.00 |
| 3 | $ 0.00 | $25.00 |
| 4 | $ 0.00 | $25.00 |
| 5 | $ 0.00 | $25.00 |
| 6 | $ 0.00 | $25.00 |
| 7 | $ 0.00 | $25.00 |

---

[2]While NPV and DCF are used almost interchangeably, in fact the DCF method produces an NPV.

[3]The method I reintroduce later in this chapter, the payback period, was an important analytical first step towards a rational determination of the question.

[4]Cost of capital is usually determined as a weighted average cost of capital which takes into account all sources of funds utilized by the firm.

discounted to their current value using that cost of capital.[5] He called the difference between the costs and the discounted value the net present value or NPV of a project. John Keynes, in his 1936 book, *The General Theory of Employment Interest and Money*, said that there exists an interest rate or cost of capital which deflates future profits so that they exactly equal current costs. He called this interest rate the internal rate of return or IRR. When the NPV is calculated using the IRR as the firm's cost of capital, the NPV equals zero.[6]

The data in Table 10.1 are analyzed to produce NPV and IRR values. Assuming that the firm's cost of capital is 12 percent, the data in Table 10.1 yields an NPV of $2.49. The NPV method produces a discounted profit stream of $102.49 which, after subtracting the investment's cost of $100.00, yields a discounted net return of $2.49. Providing consistent results with the NPV calculation, the IRR method calculates that the project has a rate of return of 12.98 percent, which is close to the 12-percent cost of capital. With a lower cost of capital, say 10 percent, the project has an NPV of $8.07 in current net dollars; it still has an IRR of 12.98 percent, since changing the firm's cost of capital does not affect the project's IRR. Returning to the original cost of capital, 12 percent, the firm would pursue a project whose NPV is greater than zero.[7] The decision process with IRR is similar; the firm would want to do a project if the IRR is greater than the firm's hurdle rate (which is its cost of capital).

If the Jones and Morrison Plush Toy Company (the firm whose data are in Table 10.1) had a second project under consideration, the NPV and IRR techniques would each allow the two projects to be compared. Suppose that the alternative project, also costing $100.00, has an NPV of $15.00 and an IRR of 15.46 percent. The alternative project has a higher NPV and a higher IRR. Jones and Morrison

---

[5]The idea behind this calculation is that the firm could borrow, at its cost of capital, money today and then repay that loan in the future when anticipated profits are earned.

[6]In certain circumstances, the two methods — NPV and IRR — provide variant answers.

[7]This statement assumes that there is not a higher-NPV, mutually exclusive (there cannot be both) alternate project.

Plush Toy Company would rank the alternate project higher than the project in Table 10.1 and, if capital was limited, would do the alternate project instead of the project in Table 10.1.

So what is wrong with NPV and IRR? As far as they go, nothing is wrong with either of them. Theirs is a problem of omission. They miss the cash impact of an investment decision on the firm. Throughout *Lead with Cash*, the idea that firms need to keep their eyes on cash and cash flow has been repeated in numerous different contexts. In capital budgeting, the problem is that if the only decision-making tool used is NPV and/or IRR, and if only positive-NPV projects are accepted, the firm may still find itself in a cash bind during periods of difficult credit or slowing sales.

Let us consider the project cost and refer to the data in Table 10.2. Even though profits are not earned in the example in Table 10.2 until year 7, this project (with a 12-percent cost of capital) has an NPV of $2.49, exactly the same as the project in Table 10.1.[8] However, the two projects exhibit completely different cash flow streams. The project in Table 10.1 throws off a steady stream of cash, while the project in Table 10.2 does not have any cash flow until the seventh year.

Table 10.2   Jones and Morrison Plush Toy Company — Project with Delayed Profitability.

| Year | Costs | Profits |
|------|-------|---------|
| 1 | $100.00 | $  0.00 |
| 2 | $  0.00 | $  0.00 |
| 3 | $  0.00 | $  0.00 |
| 4 | $  0.00 | $  0.00 |
| 5 | $  0.00 | $  0.00 |
| 6 | $  0.00 | $  0.00 |
| 7 | $  0.00 | $202.88 |

---

[8]The IRR on this project is only 12.51 percent, and not 12.98 percent as with Table 10.1. The difference between them arises from timing differences in the profit streams.

In deriving NPV, with the data in Table 10.2, the fact that there is a six-year wait for cash flows has no impact on the calculation. Both projects have the same NPV, but the first one (in Table 10.1) throws off a steady stream of cash while the second (in Table 10.2) yields no cash until the end of year 7. These are not equivalent projects, even though they have the same NPV. Clearly, the project providing steady cash flow is superior to the one with the delayed cash flow. In other words, using NPV analysis alone is not enough.

The payback method for evaluating investments is much less sophisticated than either NPV or IRR. The method merely asks how many years, given the expected stream of profits, the investor has to wait to recoup his or her investment dollars. Applying the method to the data in Tables 10.1 and 10.2 yields an answer of four years for the data in Table 10.1 ($25 multiplied by four years equals $100), and six years (when the $202.88 is received) for the data in Table 10.2. On this basis, the project in Table 10.1 is superior to the investment in Table 10.2. Recall that both projects have the same NPV. Payback argues that the first project is superior because the investor gets his or her money back quicker. This method is especially useful for two projects with the same NPV; in such a case, payback provides a valuable incremental piece of information. However, it must be recalled that payback ignores the time value of money issue entirely and does nothing to consider risk difference between projects.

Payback is also a valuable tool even when projects have different NPVs. Consider the five projects (each of which has a $100 initial investment cost) listed in Table 10.3. With just NPV figuring into the decision making, project 5 is superior to the rest due to its $22.00 NPV. If, for some reason, project 5 was undoable, then project 3 would be the best given its $18.00 NPV. One way to combine the NPV and payback information contained in the two columns of Table 10.3 is with a scatter plot such as the one drawn in Fig. 10.1. Within the figure, there are two clear channels of projects: the ones in the upper right-hand corner which have higher NPVs but longer payback periods, and those in the lower left-hand corner which have lower NPVs but shorter payback periods.

Table 10.3    Projects with Equal Investment
Costs But Various NPVs and Paybacks.

| Project | NPV | Payback (Years) |
|---------|---------|-----------------|
| 1 | $15.00 | 0.5 |
| 2 | $11.00 | 3 |
| 3 | $18.00 | 10 |
| 4 | $ 9.00 | 4 |
| 5 | $22.00 | 11 |

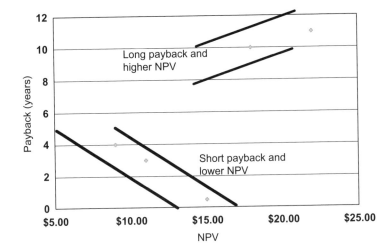

Fig. 10.1    Scatter Plot: NPV vs. Payback (Using Data from Table 10.3).

When the two techniques, NPV and payback, are viewed together, the simple, clear-cut decision rule of choosing the project with the highest NPV or the one with the shortest payback vanishes. Instead, the analyst bifurcates the problem to decide whether a higher NPV or a shorter payback is preferred. Within the high NPV range (the upper right-hand side of the figure), project 3 with the lower NPV but the shorter payback would probably be chosen. In the short payback range (the lower left-hand side of the figure), project 1 clearly dominates because it gives the highest NPV and the shortest payback.

Choosing between project 3 (the winner in the high-NPV range) and project 1 (the winner in the short-payback-period range) is more

Table 10.4    Discounted Payback: 12-Percent Cost of Capital, $100 Initial Investment Cost.

| Year | Cash Flow | Discounted Cash Flow | Cumulative Discounted Cash Flow |
|------|-----------|----------------------|---------------------------------|
| 1 | $25.00 | $22.32 | — |
| 2 | $25.00 | $19.93 | $ 42.25 |
| 3 | $25.00 | $17.79 | $ 60.05 |
| 4 | $25.00 | $15.89 | $ 75.93 |
| 5 | $25.00 | $14.19 | $ 90.12 |
| 6 | $25.00 | $12.67 | $102.79 |

problematic. Companies with limited credit availability or forthcoming repayment problems would probably move towards the short-payback-range option.

An imperfect solution, though better than just the simple payback method, called discounted payback analysis, introduces elements of NPV into the simple payback calculation. Discounted payback is calculated by using the firm's cost of capital to discount future profits back to their current value. Table 10.4 performs a discounted payback analysis using the data from Table 10.1.

Normal payback analysis says that the $100 project returns all of the investor's funds after four years (4 × $25). Discounted payback analysis discounts the cash flows received each year to reflect the impact of the time value of money. In that case, the payback period for the investment in Table 10.4 occurs during the sixth year (and not the fourth year), when the discounted total of $100 is finally received.

This book does not aim to disparage either NPV or IRR. In fact, they are wonderful tools which provide critical guidance in difficult business situations. Instead, the hope is that readers understand that NPV and IRR alone are not enough. Readers need to consider how and when an investment returns cash. Strong, well-diversified companies may be able to ignore the pleas to consider how every investment affects their future cash levels. All other companies would benefit by considering discounted payback along with either NPV or IRR.

# 11. The Impact of Leverage: Examining Private Equity*

The first wave of highly leveraged transactions (HLTs), also known as leveraged buyouts (LBOs), began in the late 1980s. Fewer transactions occurred in the 1990s after a number of companies in the first wave failed when the economy slowed down. More recently, the driving force behind leveraged deals has been the private equity business. Private equity has grown exponentially in the past decade. In the U.S., an unprecedented takeover binge occurred in 2005–2007 as private equity firms used leveraged loans (at the same time that subprime borrowers used No Income No Assets loans to buy houses) to finance numerous transactions. Consider how a major player in the industry, Sun Capital Partners, Inc. (SCP), described itself on its website in 2008 (bold font added by the author):

> Sun Capital Partners, Inc. is a leading private investment firm focused on leveraged buyouts, equity, debt, and other investments in market-leading companies that can benefit from its in-house operating professionals and experience. Sun Capital affiliates invest in companies which typically have the number one or two market position in their industry, long-term competitive advantages, and significant barriers to entry.... 
>
> Sun Capital affiliates have invested in and managed **more than 190 companies** worldwide since Sun Capital's **inception in 1995**, with combined **sales in excess of $40 billion**

*Article reprinted with permission from the publisher, The Berkeley Electronic Press, ©2009. Originally published in *Journal of Business Valuation and Economic Loss Analysis*, available at http://www.bepress.com/jbvela/.

and more than **150,000 employees**. On a consolidated basis, Sun Capital's affiliated portfolio companies would rank in the top 100 of Fortune Magazine's listing of the 500 largest companies in the United States.

Sun Capital has approximately $10 billion of equity capital under management, and can invest more than $2 billion of capital in any one transaction. Sun Capital often **bridges the entire purchase price at closing**; raising permanent debt financing afterwards. Sun Capital is one of the very few private equity firms that has completed all transactions to which it has committed, despite the difficult economic and financing environment in 2007, and thus far in 2008.[1]

Companies such as SCP are important players in American business. Using their estimate of a US$10 billion equity capital investment and an 80-percent debt ratio suggests that SCP controls companies worth approximately US$50 billion. Analyzing this development from a societal point of view requires that we understand whether SCP has in fact shared its "operating professionals and experience" with the enterprises and thereby improved their results, or whether SCP has merely increased the acquired companies' debt load and, using a portfolio concept, is willing to let the strong excel and the weak fail. More is said about this idea later in this chapter.

Doug Lowenstein, President of the Private Equity Council, noted in a speech that the private equity industry, which had raised US$5 billion in capital in 2002, was able to expand that amount to US$198 billion in 2006.[2] The reach of the industry is exemplified by the announcement that a company owned by Blackstone, a large American private equity firm, was in talks to acquire the Viennese giant Ferris wheel. The nationalistic political party in Austria, the Austrian Freedom Party, has attacked the proposed transaction.

Besides the issue of whether private equity funds can profitably invest hundreds of billions of dollars, the sheer amount of money involved in private equity raises a host of societal issues. Amongst these are employment questions (will private equity owners be less

---

[1]Source: http://www.suncappart.com/, Overview section, May 30, 2008.
[2]Columbia Business School Private Equity and Venture Capital Club, *The Carried Interest*, Vol. 1, 2008, p. 1.

compassionate?), the concentration of ownership (will private equity owners destroy economic competition?), and the shrouding of critical company decisions from public view (e.g., will private equity firms be unwilling to address environmental issues?).

How private equity firms value their acquisitions is a key question.[3] The simplest, and probably the most common, technique used to value target companies is an earnings-multiple method. This technique usually relies on an earnings figure called earnings before interest, taxes, depreciation, and amortization (EBITDA). EBITDA equals operating income plus depreciation and amortization, as seen in equation (11.1).

$$\text{EBITDA} = \text{Operating income (EBIT)}$$
$$+ \text{Depreciation and Amortization.} \quad (11.1)$$

Operating income equals operating revenues less operating costs. Operating costs include cost of goods sold; selling, general, and administrative (SGA) expenses; and depreciation and amortization. Depreciation and amortization are added back to EBIT because they are non-cash expenses which are available for use by the private equity firm.

Private equity companies buy firms (either public or private companies) at a multiple of their EBITDA value. Depending on the target's size, profit margin, industry, and other factors, the multiple might range between 3 and 10. The purchase price is paid for with a mix of equity and debt. Typically, private equity firms lever up their acquisitions beyond the level that the company was historically levered and beyond the norm of other firms in the industry. One explanation for introducing high leverage is that it forces a company to stay focused on improvement, growth, and profits.[4] While the private equity firm owns a company, it seeks improvement in the firm's performance by fixing its infrastructure, compensation

---

[3]I have greatly benefited from discussions with Bill Haan and Tom McCarthy on this and other topics.
[4]Michael Jensen made this point in his presidential address before the American Finance Association meeting, published in the *Journal of Finance*, 1993, pp. 831–880.

plan, management, marketing and sales methods, and other areas of weakness. By achieving these, the company's revenues increase while its costs decrease; consequently, its EBITDA increases. The private equity firm then profits when it sells the firm, since its value rises along with its EBITDA.[5] It is also conceivable that the company may command a higher multiple following the changes, which also raises the purchase price. One reason for a higher multiple may be that the firm's growth rate has increased following changes initiated by the private equity firm. Another reason may be that the firm is now more highly leveraged than it had been previously (more on this below).

This process of value creation is described mathematically below:

$$\text{Enterprise value} - \text{Debt} = \text{Equity value.} \qquad (11.2)$$

$$\text{Enterprise value} = \text{Multiple} \times \text{EBITDA.} \qquad (11.3)$$

Increases in either the EBITDA or the multiple (equation (11.3)) raise enterprise value, which after the repayment of debt increases the firm's equity value (equation (11.2)).

Among the firms acquired in the recent private equity buyout binge were many in which erstwhile rational people paid huge premiums, sometimes approaching 50 percent, above market prices for companies. Many of these deals were done at earnings-multiples greater than 10 times EBITDA. Table 11.1 illustrates this point using nine prominent transactions.

The TXU buyout of shareholders, for example, cost US$32 billion plus the assumption of US$13 billion in debt. The buyers were private equity firms Texas Pacific Group and Kohlberg Kravis Roberts, and a partner, Goldman Sachs. The 25-percent equity premium (see Table 11.1) meant that the group paid US$6.4 billion more than the "efficient" stock market thought TXU was worth. How could this be? Was the stock market incorrect? Were the buyout firms imprudent?

A year after Blackstone's 2007 acquisition of the Hilton hotel chain, a lot had changed: the real estate market had fallen from

---

[5]Some private equity firms (particularly larger ones) pay dividends to themselves after completing a purchase. They use new debt to fund the dividend.

Table 11.1   Nine Major Private Equity Deals (2005–2007).

| Company | Year | Premium to Market |
|---|---|---|
| SunGard | 2005 | 44% |
| Kinder Morgan | 2006 | 27% |
| Clear Channel Communications | 2006 | 30% |
| Harrah's Entertainment, Inc. | 2006 | 36% |
| PETCO Animal Supplies, Inc. | 2006 | 49% |
| TXU | 2007 | 25% |
| First Data | 2007 | 26% |
| Hilton | 2007 | 32% |
| Equity Office Properties | 2007 | 37% |

lofty heights, high gasoline prices were scaring people into staying at home, and hotel room rates were in decline. As reported in *The New York Times*, the value of a still-public competitor, Starwoods Hotels & Resorts, had fallen over the time period by 45 percent.[6] It is highly likely that the value of Hilton had fallen too. Presumably, the US$5.17 billion that Blackstone had invested of its own money was worth less a year later.

Many announced private equity deals fell through in 2008 when the money spigot (bank lenders) shut. How the target companys' stock fared after the deals died may also illustrate the precarious pricing models employed in some private equity transactions. For example, Penn National Gaming, Inc. agreed to be acquired by Fortress Investment Group and Centerbridge Partners for US$67 per share. After the demise of the deal, the stock traded at US$27.06 per share on July 10, 2008.

In some cases, after the acquisition buyout, firms change management teams and instill the company with a new spirit of creativity along with lean management. Maybe their plan is to "lead with cash flow". Organic growth and profit improvement do lead to a higher valuation. Is it reasonable to anticipate a valuation surge in excess of 34 percent (the simple unweighted average of the

---

[6]See Cyrus Sanati, "High-Water Mark," *The New York Times*, July 4, 2008.

equity premiums paid in Table 11.1)? Could current management be so incompetent as to not be aware of growth and cost-saving opportunities?

Central to modern finance theory is the concept of market efficiency. In its basic form, market efficiency means that a stock's price fully reflects *all* the available information about it, its industry, and the global economy. While there is no agreement on what the market price should be today — some investors are long in the stock while others are short — the price reflects all that is known about the company. Finance professionals do not say that the price is accurate, though market efficiency purists might go that far. What they do say is that prices are unpredictable, which may seem counterintuitive. Unpredictability means that since everything has been reflected in the current price (with some investors going long and others going short), changes from that price are not predictable events.

Another explanation for the high premiums paid to shareholders in buyouts is that there is a transactions-based mentality to the private equity industry and its pricing model. Many private equity firms are paid annual management fees that are unrelated to the overall success of their investments. The typical private equity model is a 2/20, split, with the investor paying 2 percent of their investment to the private equity firm each year as a management fee and then paying the firm an additional 20 percent of realized profits. Under the transactions model, it is in the private equity firm's best interest to spend all of an existing fund's money to justify raising another fund and more money. If this is an accurate representation, there need not be a close relationship between purchase price and actual value because then fund objectives are not aligned with those of its investors.

In fact, most of the cast of characters in a private equity transaction make out well. The list includes the fund's partners, institutional investors, the existing public company's management and shareholders, and holders of the original debt in the acquired firm. How does each benefit from taking a public company private? The private equity firm itself is probably the biggest winner because it has nothing to lose under a 2/20 compensation model. Each year, it earns 2 percent of the fund's invested capital, regardless of the performance of the portfolio of companies owned by the fund. Most funds are contractually obligated to close out their investments within 10 or 12 years. At that point, the institutional and other investors determine whether the private equity firm has earned them a sufficient return in comparison with alternative investments. Existing shareholders and management are rewarded immediately with a share price surge and, in the case of managers, with exit or retention bonuses. A possible immediate loser may be the holders of the original company's debt obligations, who, unless they had sufficient covenant protection, might find themselves either subordinated to secured loans issued to finance the buyout or else on par with other loans taken on either at the time of investment or later when the private equity firm pays itself an outsized dividend.

Still another answer to the pricing conundrum may simply be the impact of leverage on firm value. To understand the movement to take companies private, to conduct leveraged recapitalizations, or to use excess cash to buy back shares, let us first see how these tactics theoretically lead to value creation. A common first step after purchasing a company is for a private equity firm to change its capital structure. The new capital structure contains more debt (and consequently less equity) than when the firm was public. How this capital structure change affects the firm's weighted average cost of capital (WACC) is at the crux of the valuation puzzle. Note, of course, that if the acquired firm is later resold by the private equity firm with a capital structure similar to the one it originally had, there is no value creation. Presumably, the resale occurs at a leverage rate between the firm's original low debt ratio and the private equity firm's imposed high debt ratio.

WACC is used throughout the finance profession as a measure of the cost of capital to a firm. The basic formula is seen in equation (11.4).

$$\text{WACC} = \alpha_d(1 - T)r_d + (1 - \alpha_d)r_e, \qquad (11.4)$$

where

$\alpha_d$ = debt portion of firm's capital structure
$T$ = tax rate
$r_d$ = cost of debt
$r_e$ = cost of equity.

As the private equity firm increases the leverage on the newly acquired company, its WACC declines since $r_d$ is generally less than $r_e$ and $(1-T)$, which represents the tax deductibility of debt financing, further heightens this cost advantage. A lower WACC, in the simplest of worlds, leads to an increase in the firm's value derived from its future cash flows. This is illustrated in Table 11.2 for the case of an acquisition which has rising future cash flows, a case with falling future cash flows, and a case with constant future cash flows. In all three instances, the value of the firm grows dramatically. At the bottom of each of the three cases is a ratio that compares the value of the original firm to that of the highly levered firm analog. While it is true that the best outcome derives from the case with rising cash flows (the value of the firm rises by 64.5 percent and the value of each levered share increases by 416.8 percent), with constant and falling cash flows, the more highly levered firm also achieves a substantial valuation premium over the less levered firm, though to a lesser extent. Moreover, to be ultraconservative, the analysis assumes no future growth in the calculation of the terminal value for years beyond the first three shown in the table. That is, the impact of levering up the company is still greater if in fact the company experiences any growth after the third year of the analysis.

Merton Miller and Franco Modigliani, who received Nobel Prizes in 1990 and 1985, respectively, produced the seminal work on the question of the impact of leverage on value.[7] They theorized that, in a world without taxes and no bankruptcy costs, regardless of how a firm finances itself (what is known as its capital structure), its value remains unchanged. They argued that, no matter how a pie is

---

[7]See Franco Modigliani and Merton Miller, "The Cost of Capital, Corporation Finance and the Theory of Investment," *American Economic Review*, Vol. 48, No. 3, 1958, pp. 261–297.

Table 11.2   The Impact of Higher Leverage on Valuation: Rising, Falling, and Constant Income Cases.

**Existing Company with Rising Cash Flow**

| | | | | TV with g = 0 |
|---|---|---|---|---|
| EBIT | 2.000 | 4.000 | 6.000 | |
| Interest | 0.360 | 0.396 | 0.468 | |
| EAT | 0.984 | 2.162 | 3.319 | |
| Depreciation | 1.000 | 1.000 | 1.000 | |
| Cash flows | 1.984 | 3.162 | 4.319 | 4.319 |
| Terminal value | | | | 45.561 |
| Cost D | 0.060 | 0.060 | 0.060 | 0.060 |
| Cost E | 0.120 | 0.120 | 0.120 | 0.120 |
| WACC | 0.095 | 0.095 | 0.095 | 0.095 |
| Discount factor | 0.913 | 0.834 | 0.762 | 0.762 |
| Discounted CF | 1.812 | 2.638 | 3.292 | 3.292 |
| Total discounted value | 42.463 | | | 34.721 |
| Total assets | 20.000 | 22.000 | 26.000 | |
| Debt | 0.300 | 0.300 | 0.300 | 0.300 |
| Equity | 0.700 | 0.700 | 0.700 | 0.700 |
| Equity value | $36.46 | | | |
| Equity value/share | $36.46 | | | |
| Ratio of values | 1.645 | | | |

**Levered Company with Rising Cash Flow**

| | | | | TV with g = 0 |
|---|---|---|---|---|
| EBIT | 2.000 | 4.000 | 6.000 | |
| Interest | 0.960 | 1.056 | 1.248 | |
| EAT | 0.624 | 1.766 | 2.851 | |
| Depreciation | 1.000 | 1.000 | 1.000 | |
| Cash flows | 1.624 | 2.766 | 3.851 | 3.851 |
| Terminal value | | | | 72.939 |
| Cost D | 0.060 | 0.060 | 0.060 | 0.060 |
| Cost E | 0.120 | 0.120 | 0.120 | 0.120 |
| WACC | 0.053 | 0.053 | 0.053 | 0.053 |
| Discount factor | 0.950 | 0.902 | 0.857 | 0.857 |
| Discounted CF | 1.543 | 2.496 | 3.300 | 3.300 |
| Total discounted value | 69.845 | | | 62.506 |
| Total assets | 20.000 | 22.000 | 26.000 | |
| Debt | 0.800 | 0.800 | 0.800 | 0.800 |
| Equity | 0.200 | 0.200 | 0.200 | 0.200 |
| Equity value | $53.85 | | | |
| Equity value/share | $188.46 | | | |
| Ratio of values | 5.168 | | | |

(*Continued*)

Table 11.2  (Continued)

| | Existing Company with Falling Cash Flow | | | | Levered Company with Falling Cash Flow | | | |
|---|---|---|---|---|---|---|---|---|
| | 6.000 | 4.000 | 2.000 | TV with g = 0 | 6.000 | 4.000 | 2.000 | TV with g = 0 |
| EBIT | 6.000 | 4.000 | 2.000 | | 6.000 | 4.000 | 2.000 | |
| Interest | 0.360 | 0.324 | 0.288 | | 0.960 | 0.864 | 0.768 | |
| EAT | 3.384 | 2.206 | 1.027 | | 3.024 | 1.882 | 0.739 | |
| Depreciation | 1.000 | 1.000 | 1.000 | | 1.000 | 1.000 | 1.000 | |
| Cash flows | 4.384 | 3.206 | 2.027 | 2.027 | 4.024 | 2.882 | 1.739 | 1.739 |
| Terminal value | | | | 21.384 | | | | 32.939 |
| Cost D | 0.060 | 0.060 | 0.060 | 0.060 | 0.060 | 0.060 | 0.060 | 0.060 |
| Cost E | 0.120 | 0.120 | 0.120 | 0.120 | 0.120 | 0.120 | 0.120 | 0.120 |
| WACC | 0.095 | 0.095 | 0.095 | 0.053 | 0.053 | 0.053 | 0.053 | 0.053 |
| Discount factor | 0.913 | 0.834 | 0.762 | 0.762 | 0.950 | 0.902 | 0.857 | 0.857 |
| Discounted CF | 4.004 | 2.674 | 1.545 | 1.545 | 3.822 | 2.600 | 1.490 | 1.490 |
| Total discounted value | 24.520 | | | 16.296 | 36.140 | | | 28.228 |
| Total assets | 20.000 | 18.000 | 16.000 | | 20.000 | 18.000 | 16.000 | |
| Debt | 0.300 | 0.300 | 0.300 | 0.800 | 0.800 | 0.800 | 0.800 | 0.800 |
| Equity | 0.700 | 0.700 | 0.700 | 0.200 | 0.200 | 0.200 | 0.200 | 0.200 |
| Equity value | $8.52 | | | | $20.14 | | | |
| Equity value/ share | $18.52 | | | | $70.49 | | | |
| Ratio of values | 1.474 | | | | 3.806 | | | |

(Continued)

Table 11.2    (*Continued*)

### Existing Company with Steady Cash Flow

| | | | | TV with g = 0 |
|---|---|---|---|---|
| EBIT | 4.000 | 4.000 | 4.000 | |
| Interest | 0.360 | 0.360 | 0.360 | |
| EAT | 2.184 | 2.184 | 2.184 | |
| Depreciation | 1.000 | 1.000 | 1.000 | |
| Cash flows | 3.184 | 3.184 | 3.184 | 3.184 |
| Terminal value | | | | 33.586 |
| Cost D | 0.060 | 0.060 | 0.060 | 0.060 |
| Cost E | 0.120 | 0.120 | 0.120 | 0.120 |
| WACC | 0.095 | 0.095 | 0.095 | 0.095 |
| Discount factor | 0.913 | 0.834 | 0.762 | 0.762 |
| Discounted CF | 2.908 | 2.656 | 2.426 | 25.595 |
| Total discounted value | 33.586 | | | |
| Total assets | 20.000 | 20.000 | 20.000 | |
| Debt | 0.300 | 0.300 | 0.300 | |
| Equity | 0.700 | 0.700 | 0.700 | |
| Equity value | $27.59 | | | |
| Equity value/ share | $27.59 | | | |
| Ratio of values | 1.592 | | | |

### Levered Company with Steady Cash Flow

| | | | | TV with g = 0 |
|---|---|---|---|---|
| EBIT | 4.000 | 4.000 | 4.000 | |
| Interest | 0.960 | 0.960 | 0.960 | 0.960 |
| EAT | 1.824 | 1.824 | 1.824 | 1.824 |
| Depreciation | 1.000 | 1.000 | 1.000 | 1.000 |
| Cash flows | 2.824 | 2.824 | 2.824 | 2.824 |
| Terminal value | | | | 53.485 |
| Cost D | 0.060 | 0.060 | 0.060 | 0.060 |
| Cost E | 0.120 | 0.120 | 0.120 | 0.120 |
| WACC | 0.053 | 0.053 | 0.053 | 0.053 |
| Discount factor | 0.950 | 0.902 | 0.857 | 0.857 |
| Discounted CF | 2.682 | 2.548 | 2.420 | 45.835 |
| Total discounted value | 53.485 | | | |
| Total assets | 20.000 | 20.000 | 20.000 | |
| Debt | 0.800 | 0.800 | 0.800 | |
| Equity | 0.200 | 0.200 | 0.200 | |
| Equity value | $37.48 | | | |
| Equity value/ share | $131.20 | | | |
| Ratio of values | 4.756 | | | |

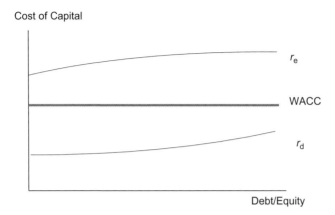

Fig. 11.1   WACC — Modigliani and Miller Theory (No Taxes): Demonstrating the Value-Invariance Principle.

sliced, there is only so much of the pie to go around. This is known as the value-invariance principle. The principle argues that financing decisions and the value of the firm are independent.

The graphical view of the Modigliani and Miller (M&M) theory in Fig. 11.1 shows the tradeoff between a firm's cost of money (WACC) and its debt/equity ratio. Basically, the theory says that as the firm takes on more debt (i.e., as its debt/equity ratio rises), the costs of both debt ($r_d$) and equity ($r_e$) increase. These costs increase because the heightened use of debt raises the firm's risk, since there is a greater chance that it will not be able to pay the interest owed on the debt or repay the principal. Consequently, debt holders demand a higher return and shareholders require a higher return on their capital. Yet, the WACC remains constant in Fig. 11.1 due to the fact that $r_d < r_e$. In other words, two things are happening: (1) both $r_d$ and $r_e$ increase due to the firm's increased riskiness given its higher debt ratio; and (2) the WACC does not change because the movement towards relatively lower-cost debt is *exactly* balanced by the increasing costs of both debt and equity. In this version of the M&M theory (without taxes), a higher debt ratio is not a costless route to an increase in firm value.

What happens when the theory is made more realistic by relaxing the no-tax assumption? In that case, according to the theory, the value of the firm depends on how it is financed. Driving this

conclusion is the tax deductibility of interest paid to debt holders from income before taxes are calculated. In other words, funds
raised from debt financing are subsidized by the government because
returns paid to bond holders reduce the amount of taxes owed to
the government. Using equation (11.4) above, WACC decreases as
the proportion of debt ($\alpha_d$) increases. That is, there is an inverse
relationship between WACC and $\alpha_d$. A firm financed entirely with
debt has a WACC equal to $r_d$ $(1 - T)$, while a firm with all-equity
financing has a WACC of $r_e$. Even if $r_d = r_e$, the all-debt firm has
a clear WACC advantage due to taxes; if $r_d < r_e$, the advantage is
even greater. Figure 11.2 illustrates how the firm's WACC declines
as the debt/equity ratio rises.

The contrast between the behavior of the WACC depicted in
Figs. 11.1 and 11.2, as the firm increases its debt ratio, is the force
driving the dramatically different estimates of firm value seen above
in Table 11.2. Private equity and similarly highly leveraged transactions are partially justified by analyses which contend that the use
of debt "magically" raises valuation. Might these studies be missing
something?

The private equity firm discussed earlier, SCP, has experienced
rougher going recently. Propelled by investor capital, SCP averaged
over one transaction a month since its inception in 1995. However,
in early 2008, three of its companies filed for bankruptcy: Wickes

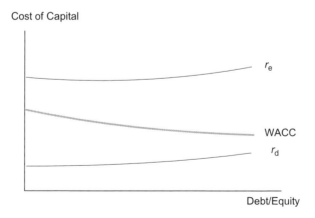

Fig. 11.2   WACC — Modigliani and Miller Theory (with Taxes).

Furniture Co., Sharper Image Corp., and Lillian Vernon Corp. Then, later in 2008, its Jevic Holding Corp. filed for bankruptcy, followed in July by its Mervyns department store. Could SCP (and other private equity firms like it) have overreached itself? A number of the companies that it owns have failed and filed for bankruptcy court protection. Possibly these failures resulted from the economic slowdown in 2008 following the unraveling of the credit market in 2007. Alternatively, SCP has discovered that if you pay too much, whoever you may be, your investment may not be able to support the level of debt that private equity firms pile on to capital structures. Of course, SCP might simply be relying on holding a large portfolio of companies, some of which do well, some of which do fine, and others of which do poorly.

The M&M theory is not silent on bankruptcy and the costs of financial distress. Rather, most analysts say that at some point, when the debt ratio is high, the firm begins to have a probability of going bankrupt.[8] Bankruptcy imposes a number of costly, nonfunctional expenses on the firm, such as legal expenses, trustee fees, costs associated with the plan of reorganization, and the loss of business due to the stigma. These costs lower the value of the firm. The probability that the firm will actually need to pay these costs depends, among other things, on its debt ratio. As the debt ratio rises, the probability of bankruptcy rises and the expected value of bankruptcy costs increases. This expected value reduces the present value of future cash flows. Consequently, debt financing has additional costs beyond the payment of interest and principal. These costs reduce the gains from tax savings arising from debt financing. This is usually called the tradeoff theorem. As seen in Fig. 11.3, at some level of the debt ratio, the decrease in WACC ends due to costs associated with a potential bankruptcy. When the WACC begins to turn up, the company is at its optimal capital structure.

---

[8]One of the earliest academic discussions of bankruptcy cost was by Nevins D. Baxter, "Leverage, Risk of Ruin and the Cost of Capital," *The Journal of Finance*, Vol. 22, No. 3, 1967, pp. 395–403. Another good discussion comes from Jacques A. Schnabel, "Bankruptcy, Interest Tax Shields and 'Optimal' Capital Structure: A Cash Flow Formulation," *Managerial and Decision Economics*, Vol. 5, No. 2, 1984, pp. 116–119.

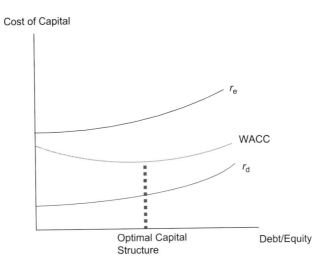

Fig. 11.3    The Tradeoff Model — With Taxes and Bankruptcy.

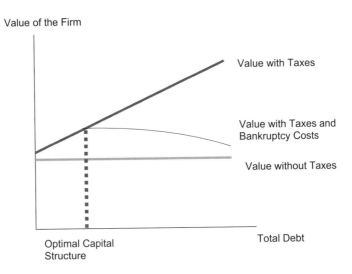

Fig. 11.4    The Value of the Firm with Different Models.

The three versions of the world discussed above are presented in a single figure, Fig. 11.4, as three value curves dependent on the amount of debt raised by the firm, rather than with debt ratios and WACCs. The lowest curve is the Modigliani and Miller case without taxes; value does not vary with the firm's level of debt. The uppermost curve shows the Modigliani and Miller world with taxes, whereby value rises with debt. The middle curve shows the value of the firm with both taxes and bankruptcy costs. The firm would probably have no debt in the first case (it would be all-equity financed), would have all debt (zero equity) in the second case, and would have a mix of debt and equity in the third case. The trick for the private equity firm is to find where the optimal capital structure point is located and to raise that level of debt. By doing so, the value of the firm is maximized.

The missing element throughout this discussion of value, capital structure, and WACC has been the price paid for the investment. Over 100 years ago, Irving Fisher[9] devised his separation theorem, which argues that the firm first makes an investment decision (whether to buy an asset and, if so, how much to pay) and then, independent of that decision, makes a financing decision (whether to use debt or equity). The key to understanding Fisher's idea is to realize that a fixed stream of cash flows can only support a certain level of debt. When a private equity firm overpays for an asset, according to Fisher, it needs to reduce the company's usage of debt to match up with the firm's cash flows. Ignoring price in the capital structure decision process is conceptually the same as ignoring financial distress or bankruptcy costs.

Bankruptcy is a legal event that has a rising probability as a firm takes on debt. In contrast, financial distress occurs when a firm is weakened by financial or operating decisions that lead to a loss in confidence in the firm by its customers, suppliers, bankers, and employees. A financially distressed firm incurs many costs that are not part of the traditional bankruptcy cost equation. For example, a financially distressed firm would likely face strict loan covenants that would impinge on its ability to grow and operate, be restricted by suppliers from normal trade credit terms, and thus would be forced to use its own capital; it might underinvest due to a shortage of capital,

---

[9]See Irving Fisher, *Nature of Capital and Income*, Macmillan, London, 1912; or Irving Fisher, *Theory of Interest*, Macmillan, London, 1930.

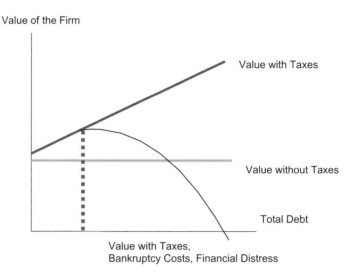

Fig. 11.5   The Value of the Firm with Different Models (with Financial Distress).

lose customers, and raise cash by selling off its assets below their true worth. Incorporating these costs into the theory might easily yield a value relationship that looks like that in Fig. 11.5.

Some analysts are uncomfortable with the view of the world expressed in Fig. 11.5, believing staunchly in the world view described in Fig. 11.4. Some academics, though, have begun to support the argument advanced in Fig. 11.5.[10] In a recent study which accounts for purchase price, a dynamic capital structure model was created which concludes that the median firm in Standard & Poor's Compustat database has an optimal capital structure of 15.29 percent, which is far below the actual capital structure of 22.62 percent. In other words, private equity activity which buys companies and raises their debt beyond 15.29 percent is pushing down value, not raising it!

---

[10]See, for example, Nengjiu Ju, Robert Parrino, Allen M. Poteshman, and Michael S. Weisbach, "Horses and Rabbits? Trade-Off Theory and Optimal Capital Structure," *Journal of Financial and Quantitative Analysis*, Vol. 40, No. 2, 2005, pp. 259–281.

# PART II

# 12. Cash Flow Basics

The day begins and Joan's Bakery has $530.02 in the till. Following the morning rush for coffee, doughnuts, and pastry, a delivery truck arrives with 14 bags of flour at about 11:00 am. Another big rush occurs as the high school lets out with students mostly buying coffee and cookies. The bakery closes up at 4:00 pm. Joan, the bakery's owner, counts the money in the till, and finds that there is only $490.34. She is confused. The register contains less than when the bakery opened that morning. How could she sell goods all day long and lose $39.68? Was one of her employees pocketing the money?

Joan's cash control is actually very good: no one handles cash at the bakery except for her. She had learned an expensive lesson the prior year from a dishonest employee. Maybe, she thinks, she is losing her mind. As she sits down with her lips scrunched up in contemplation, her young son walks in covered with flour. Then Joan remembers two things: (1) she had forgotten to put the 14 bags of flour into the storage room, and (2) she had paid cash in the amount of $280 for the flour in order to qualify for free shipping. Adding back the $280.00 to the missing $39.68, Joan is pleased to realize that the bakery's customers had paid in $240.32 during the day.

This simple scenario of a company's daily cash in and cash out provides a useful starting point to begin thinking about cash flow. The definition of cash flow, in its simplest form, is the amount of cash taken in or spent during a given time period. Other, more complex cash flow definitions are discussed in Chapter 15, including operating

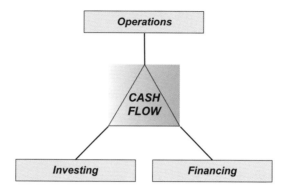

Fig. 12.1   Contributions to Cash Flow.

cash flow and free cash flow, but for now the simple definition stated here is sufficient.

Cash flow is like a bathtub that has three faucets feeding into it. Figure 12.1 illustrates this point. A company produces or spends cash in three ways.[1] The first source of cash is referred to as cash flow from operations. As the name suggests, these funds are derived from the day-to-day operations of the business. Items included in the calculation of cash flow from operations include:

- Revenues from business activities;
- Monies paid to employees;
- Monies paid to suppliers;
- Interest received or paid;
- Dividend payments from the ownership of stock; and
- Taxes paid.

Cash flow from operations is achieved by the company from its normal operations. Cash flow from operations is not the same thing as profits. There are a number of expenses that reduce company profits but which do not reduce cash flow; these include depreciation (a charge taken against capital assets), amortization (similar to

---

[1]In fact, companies also derive cash due to the effects of foreign exchange. This fourth category of cash flow is not discussed in the text in order to reduce complexity.

depreciation but used on intangible assets), and depletion (to account for the erosion of natural resources).

The second source of cash flow comes from investing activities. Here, monies received or spent on capital expenditures or investments are recorded. Items included in the calculation of cash flow from investing include:

- Monies spent purchasing plant and equipment;
- Monies received from selling plant and equipment;
- Monies lent or used to purchase other firms' debt;
- Monies received from investments in other firms' equity; and
- Monies spent to acquire equity in other firms.

This category of cash flow details cash flowing into or out of the firm as a consequence of its investing activities.

The third and final source of cash flow is from financing activities. This category accounts for the funds the firm raises or repays in order to finance its business. Items included in the calculation of cash flow from financing include:

- Monies raised or repaid from the sale of stock;
- Monies raised or repaid from the sale of debt; and
- Monies disbursed to pay dividends.

This third category of cash flow items reflects the various sources and uses of financing that the company engages in.

All public companies make available a statement of cash flows that includes these three components (plus one, when necessary, for the impact of foreign exchange). The advantage to presenting cash flow details in three parts is that it is then clear whether the cash being generated comes from activities related to the company's product/service or from its investing or financing activities. Previously, the statement of cash flows was called either the statement of changes in financial position or the flow of funds statement. The latter name is perhaps the most descriptive because a statement of cash flows reveals how funds are flowing into and out of the firm from operations, investing, and financing. Like a harbor master watching the boats come into and out of the harbor, the firm's manager needs to monitor these flows for deviations from their historical pattern or from industry norms.

The cash flow statement documents a firm's liquidity or solvency. The statement of cash flows is perhaps the best tool for analyzing a company's ability to pay its bills and to remain solvent. A firm that reports a string of profits but which simultaneously reports an outflow of cash on its statement of cash flows, for example, is a company that needs closer inspection. An important distinction between the statement of cash flows and the income statement or balance sheet is that the cash flow statement does not include the effect of non-cash transactions such as depreciation, amortization, depletion, and write-offs of overvalued assets (common ones are goodwill, inventories, deferred tax assets, and uncollectible debts). While non-cash charges represent actual reductions in value (such as the depreciation that occurs over a year when a chair is used 40 times per day), for the most part, they are charges related to expenses that occurred in prior years. For example, a chair that is depreciated this year was purchased three years ago and was depreciated in the prior two years as well.

Simply put, the three portions of cash flow describe cash generated or spent by running the business, cash generated or spent through investments, and cash acquired or spent from capital raising. The sum of the three equals the firm's net cash flow. One advantage to this breakdown is that it allows for a clear understanding of how the firm generates or sheds cash. Some companies are profitable but have shrinking cash levels, while others are unprofitable but are generating cash. The distinction may not be clear to the reader now, but it will be shown that it is of vital importance in terms of the firm's solvency and survivability. Knowing where and how a company derives its cash is the key to understanding its future financial position.

Returning once again to Joan's Bakery, discussed at the beginning of this chapter, its cash flow statement for the year is presented below. The year has been uneventful other than the fact that Joan needed to purchase a new oven for $25,000, which she financed with a loan from the local bank. The three main parts of the statement of cash flows show that Joan's had $36,000 of cash flow from operations,

$25,000 of negative cash flow from investing activities, and $25,000 of cash flow from financing. Since the investing and financing cash flows match, the year ends with Joan's Bakery having a positive cash flow of $36,000.

**Joan's Bakery**
**Consolidated Statement of Cash Flows**
**(in thousands of dollars)**

|  | 12 Months Ending Dec. 31, 2009 | |
| --- | --- | --- |
| Net Income/Starting Line | 23 | |
| Depreciation/Depletion | 15 | |
| Amortization | — | |
| Deferred Taxes | 1 | |
| Changes in Working Capital | −3 | |
| Cash from Operating Activities | | 36 |
| Capital Expenditures | −25 | |
| Cash from Investing Activities | | −25 |
| Financing Cash Flow Items | 25 | |
| Total Cash Dividends Paid | 0 | |
| Issuance (Retirement) of Stock, Net | 0 | |
| Issuance (Retirement) of Debt, Net | 0 | |
| Cash from Financing Activities | | 25 |
| Net Change in Cash | | 36 |

Note how cash flow is not the same thing as net income (profit). Joan's Bakery earned a profit of $23,000, while its cash flow was $36,000. Cash flow adds back to net income those expenditures which are non-cash in nature. The most common example of this is depreciation. Joan's Bakery had $15,000 of depreciation for the year. These depreciation expenses were deducted from revenues in the process of determining net income. Depreciation represents the loss in value of Joan's Bakery's assets (display cases, ovens, counters and chairs, and outdoor signage) due to wear and tear or the passage of time. Some firms also record depreciation to reflect the loss in value of their assets due to technological changes or obsolescence.

The statement of cash flows is generally more revealing than either the company's income statement or its balance sheet. This is particularly true when a company is generating profits but its cash flows are negative; in that case, this profitable firm may have trouble paying its bills when they come due. An extended period of positive profits and negative cash flows suggests that the company is unable to internally generate sufficient capital to support its growth needs.

It is often better to use the statement of cash flows, rather than mere profitability, when comparing two companies. In Table 12.1, Joan's Bakery is compared with her across-town rival, Mike's Bakery. Both firms had the same operating cash flow, but Mike did not invest in a new oven even though he borrowed $25,000 from the bank. While it may be true that Mike's Bakery did not need the oven, it now owns an older oven than Joan's Bakery; moreover, why did he borrow money from the bank? Was the loan needed for personal reasons (e.g., to buy a new car) or did the money go into the business (perhaps Mike raised his salary by $25,000)? Certainly doubts are raised about Mike's Bakery by a fuller examination of its finances, as seen in its statement of cash flows in Table 12.1.

Breaking apart the two bakeries' operating cash flows reveals still more discrepancies between the two enterprises in terms of their financial health and well-being (see Table 12.2). Mike's Bakery is far less profitable than Joan's. Its annual profit is only $7,000 versus Joan's $23,000. In addition, Mike's achieves its $36,000 operating

Table 12.1   Cash Flows of Joan's Bakery and Mike's Bakery (in thousands of dollars).

|  | Joan's Bakery | Mike's Bakery |
|---|---|---|
| Operating Cash Flow | 36 | 36 |
| Investing Cash Flow | −25 | 0 |
| Financing Cash Flow | 25 | 25 |

Table 12.2   Operating Cash Flows of the Two Bakeries (in thousands of dollars).

|  | Joan's Bakery | Mike's Bakery |
|---|---|---|
| Net Income/Starting Line | 23 | 7 |
| Depreciation/Depletion | 15 | 20 |
| Amortization | — | — |
| Deferred Taxes | 1 | 3 |
| Changes in Working Capital | −3 | 6 |
| Operating Cash Flow | 36 | 36 |

cash flow mostly from depreciation and changes in its working capital. The large amount of depreciation, coupled with the lack of new investment, suggests that Mike's Bakery may need to make a large investment in equipment in the future.

Negative changes in working capital, such as at Joan's Bakery, occur when a firm's current assets decrease and/or its current liabilities grow. Conversely, a positive change in working capital, such as that at Mike's Bakery, occurs when current assets increase and/or current liabilities fall. Working capital (often called net working capital) combines current assets and current liabilities by subtracting current liabilities from current assets. Current assets include items such as inventories and accounts receivable. Current liabilities include items such as accounts payable and notes payable (usually to a bank). An increase in current assets occurs when, for example, inventories rise. Current liabilities rise when, for example, bank debt increases (short-term bank loans are part of current liabilities while longer-term debt is a component of total liabilities).

Using this additional information about working capital, it is easy to understand why concerns may arise due to discrepancies between the two bakeries in changes to their working capital. For example, Joan's Bakery's fall in working capital may have happened because it received a check from the local school for a batch of cookies it previously sold to the lunch program (reducing its current assets) or because it took out a short-term loan from its local bank (raising its current liabilities). Likewise, Mike's Bakery's rise in working capital may have occurred because it has accumulated additional inventories (raising its current assets) or because it repaid its suppliers (reducing its current liabilities). Although the overall conclusion is not unequivocal, it is likely that Mike's Bakery is weaker than Joan's Bakery, at least regarding changes in their working capital.

## A More Complex Measure of Cash Flow

The simple measure of cash flow used so far in this chapter is sufficient for most analytical purposes. If the reader is going to learn one additional cash flow measure, it should be free cash flow (note that Chapter 15 discusses a number of different cash flow measures in great depth). Free cash flow equals cash flow from operations minus the firm's capital expenditures.[2] Capital expenditures, or CAPEX, are monies spent to acquire assets with a life longer than a year. The CAPEX deducted from cash flow from operations to obtain free cash flow should be just those funds spent to maintain existing facilities; monies spent on new assets should not be included.[3] For tax purposes, CAPEX is not deductible against revenues, but is instead capitalized or deducted gradually from income over the useful life of the asset.

The critical word in the phrase "free cash flow" is the word "free". Free cash flow identifies the amount of cash available to the firm after it pays its operating bills (deducted from revenue to arrive at net income) and spends monies on CAPEX to maintain its existing operations. For public companies, data on the size of CAPEX are found in the statement of cash flows within the investing section. Unfortunately, few of these companies separate out the portion of CAPEX used to maintain existing assets and the portion invested in new assets. Consequently, most analysts deduct the entire CAPEX amount in determining cash flow, even though their calculation is too conservative.

The two principal differences between net income and free cash flow concern the treatment of investment goods and working capital. Regarding the first item, the net income calculation takes out depreciation as an expense. In contrast, the free cash flow calculation takes out CAPEX. In a steady-state world where CAPEX is exactly equal to depreciation, this difference between net income and free cash flow vanishes. However, few companies reach a steady state, though, when forecasting into the long term, it is not unreasonable to expect companies to eventually reach a steady state.

---

[2]If the purpose is to determine the free cash flow to the firm, as opposed to free cash flow to the firm's owners, then it is necessary to add back the after-tax interest paid by the company to its creditors.

[3]Some analysts argue that if the new investment is required to remain competitive and stay in business, then that investment too should be taken out of cash flow from operations to arrive at free cash flow.

Changes in net working capital, you will recall, arise from company decisions regarding their current assets and current liabilities. Free cash flow removes changes in net working capital. In contrast, net income ignores changes in net working capital. Some analysts might argue that this difference alone is sufficient to prefer free cash flow over net income, since most companies experience changes in their working capital. Rapidly growing companies typically experience rising working capital needs, while stagnant firms experience falling working capital needs. Free cash flow captures these effects on a company's cash position, while net income ignores them.

## Cash Through Different Eyes

Cash flow is the critical metric for all businesses. The simple comparison above between the two bakeries highlights the power of cash flow to impart critical information about a company's well-being. What makes cash flow an attractive analytical tool is how it focuses on the difference between money at the start and end of the period, and how it highlights the source of those funds. In the final analysis, the evaluation of corporate performance is really just that: has the firm grown its cash?

Another powerful way to view a company's cash is via the cash conversion cycle. The cash conversion cycle examines the linkage between the transactions that a company makes in the course of creating and selling its product/service. Generally, the sequence of actions starts with a company ordering raw materials and, after a series of intervening steps, ends with the company receiving cash for its product/service. Like cash flow, the cash conversion cycle measures the flow of cash into and out of a business. But with the cash conversion cycle, the view is restricted to just that segment of the business involved with the immediate production of goods/services. Sometimes the cash conversion cycle is called the time factor.[4] By

---

[4]For further discussion of the time factor and cash conversion cycle, see Harlan D. Platt, *Why Companies Fail*, Lexington Books, Lexington, MA, 1985 (reprinted by Beard Books Inc., Washington, D.C., 1999).

The company buys raw material.

The company builds a product.

The company pays suppliers, workers, etc.

The company sells the product.

The company collects money from customers.

Fig. 12.2    The Cash Conversion Cycle.[5]

shortening its time factor, a company strengthens itself financially. Therefore, when comparing two companies, the one with the shorter time factor (all other things being equal) is the healthier firm.

---

[5]These pictures come from the royalty-free site: http://www.free-pictures-photos.com/.

Think of the cash conversion cycle using the sequence of pictorial events shown in Fig. 12.2. A typical firm starts the cash conversion cycle by buying raw material inventories, which it then turns into finished goods using its labor force, equipment, utility services, and other inputs. The firm pays its suppliers relatively early if it takes advantage of discounts offered by suppliers to induce early repayment (discount terms may require repayment in as few as five days or less), or later if the firm drags out its repayment schedule to the maximum point (repayment may occur after 45 or more days). Finished goods are usually sold to customers on credit and consequently the firm does not immediately collect its cash after making a sale. At some point in the future, the firm's account receivable (the credit sale to its customer) is repaid and the cash conversion cycle ends.

Generally speaking, a firm should try to minimize its cash conversion cycle. A shorter cycle means that the firm needs working capital funds for fewer days. Having your capital tied up for 30 days is worse than having it tied up for 20 days. A 30-day cycle can only be replicated 12 times a year; in contrast, a 20-day cycle can be replicated 18 times a year. A firm that buys raw materials inventory (of a fixed size) 18 times and then turns it into product and earns a profit 18 times is clearly better off than an otherwise identical firm that can only produce product 12 times a year. However, it may be prudent to relax the goal of minimizing the cash conversion cycle if suppliers offer generous terms for early repayment (early repayment lengthens the cash conversion cycle). For example, taking a 3-percent early discount to pay bills after 5 days instead of 30 days is equivalent to earning roughly a 44-percent rate of return on investment: $365 \text{ days}/(30 \text{ days} - 5 \text{ days}) \times 3 \text{ percent} = 43.8$ percent. Such a high return is earned because the 3-percent discount (or profit) can be taken over and over again: $365 \text{ days}/(30 \text{ days} - 5 \text{ days}) = 14.6$ times per year. The company would trade off the 44-percent gain from an early repayment of its bills against the lower profitability it would achieve by having a longer time factor.

The cash conversion cycle has three principal parts:

(1) An inventory conversion period (in days);
(2) A receivables collection period (in days); and
(3) A payables deferral period (in days).

The cash conversion cycle equals the sum of the inventory conversion period plus the receivables collection period minus the payables deferral period:

$$\text{Cash conversion cycle} = \text{inventory conversion period}$$
$$+ \text{receivables collection period}$$
$$- \text{payables deferral period.} \quad (12.1)$$

This explains why a quicker repayment of an account payable lengthens the cash conversion cycle.

Using the data in Table 12.3, the cash conversion cycle is calculated straightforwardly. The inventory conversion period measures the number of days that elapse between when a company acquires its new materials inventory and when it sells its product/service. The inventory conversion period is measured by dividing the company's inventory (on its balance sheet) by its average daily sales. For example, a company with $1,500,000 of inventory and $50,000 of daily sales has a 30-day inventory conversion period.

The receivables collection period measures the length of time it takes the firm, on average, to collect its receivables. Similar to the inventory conversion period, the receivables collection period is measured by dividing the firm's accounts receivable (on its balance sheet) by its average daily sales. A company with accounts receivable of $750,000 and $50,000 of daily sales has a 15-day receivables collection period.

Table 12.3    Calculating the Cash Conversion Cycle.

| Income Statement Details | |
|---|---:|
| Annual Sales | $18,250,000 |
| Daily Sales | $50,000 |
| Daily Cost of Goods Sold | $25,000 |
| Balance Sheet Details | |
| Inventory | $1,500,000 |
| Accounts Receivable | $750,000 |
| Accounts Payable | $500,000 |
| Inventory Conversion Period = 30 days. | |
| Receivables Collection Period = 15 days. | |
| Payables Deferral Period = 20 days. | |

The payables deferral period measures how long a firm waits, on average, before it pays for its supplies (including labor). The payables deferral period is measured by dividing the firm's accounts payable by its average daily cost of goods sold (on its income statement). Thus, a firm which has $500,000 in accounts payable (on its balance sheet) and $25,000 in daily cost of goods sold has a 20-day payables deferral period.

The firm's cash conversion cycle is obtained by combining the three calculations above:

Cash conversion cycle = 30 days + 15 days − 20 days = 25 days.

Therefore, the firm has a time factor of 25 days.

It is useful to compare the cash conversion cycle between firms in the same industry or for the same firm over time. Significant industry differences, however, make it less advisable to compare the cash conversion cycles across firms in two different industries, or between firms which do business in different countries.

## Shrinking the Cash Conversion Cycle

Companies become more valuable when they shorten their cash conversion cycle. A shorter cash conversion cycle reduces the firm's working capital needs and increases its free cash flow.[6] However, actions to shrink the cash conversion cycle that harm the firm's operations and thereby threaten its profitability are imprudent and should be avoided.

To understand how a company can shrink its cash conversion cycle, let us return to the basic definition of the cash conversion cycle:

Cash conversion cycle = inventory conversion period
+ receivables collection period
− payables deferral period.

---

[6]This statement assumes that the firm can sell the additional product made by shortening the cash conversion cycle.

Steps taken to reduce either the inventory conversion period or the receivables collection period, or to lengthen the firm's payables deferral period, all produce a shorter cash conversion cycle.

Examples of actions that reduce the inventory conversion period would be to move to a just-in-time production process (this essentially asks suppliers to hold on to the firm's inventory), step up sales while holding the level of inventory flat, purchase inventories at a lower cost, or find ways to economize on inventory holdings. Reducing the inventory conversion period is probably one of the most overlooked strategies in business. When a company gets itself into trouble, turnaround managers brought in to assist the company generally look to excess inventories as a source of cash. The normal, non-turnaround manager often fails to economize on inventory holdings, either because it is someone else's job or because he/she is spending their time on more exotic tasks.

The length of the receivables collection period depends upon the company's credit policy with its customers. A firm that uses lax or easy credit terms to boost its sales may, as a result, have a long receivables collection period. Such a firm should think carefully before modifying its credit policy (in order to reduce its receivables collection period); otherwise, it might jeopardize its franchise with its customers. By contrast, companies which have "normal" credit policies may be able to affect a reduction in their receivables collection period by offering a discount to its customers for early payment or by cutting back on the amount of credit it offers.

Depending on the number of high-quality suppliers that are available and their current disposition, it may be possible for a company to get better credit terms and thereby increase its payables deferral period. Among the techniques that companies use to induce better (longer) credit terms are to sign long-term supply contracts, agree to concentrate all of their purchases with a single supplier, and involve suppliers in their future design plans. Giving away too much financially in negotiations to extend the payables deferral period is unwise, since the savings in terms of reducing working capital needs may easily be outweighed by related costs.

A company's net operating working capital is determined by adding together its inventory and accounts receivable and then subtracting off its accounts payable, as seen in the formula below:

$$\text{Net Operating Working Capital} = \text{Inventory} + \text{Accounts Receivable} \\ - \text{Accounts Payable}.$$

Using the data in Table 12.3 yields the following net operating working capital:

$$\text{Net Operating Working Capital} = \$1,500,000 + \$750,000 - \$500,000 \\ = \$1,750,000.$$

Net operating working capital describes the investment that a firm needs to make in its current assets (partially funded by its current liabilities) in order to conduct its normal business activities.

# 13. Working Capital and Cash Flow

Working capital is an odd topic: few people express an interest in learning about it, and yet more companies go bankrupt due to a failure to manage working capital properly than due to almost any other cause. To most people, working capital is a mystery. It shouldn't be. Several chapters of *Lead with Cash* are devoted to working capital to correct this imbalance.

Working capital is neither difficult nor esoteric. Ignoring working capital at best results in a firm having less cash available, and at worst leads to the firm violating its loan covenants, being less profitable, and possibly filing for bankruptcy protection. Carefully managing a company's working capital can generate cash. For that reason, it is not possible, in my view, to have too much material in *Lead with Cash* about working capital and working capital management.

Let us start at the beginning. Companies have assets and liabilities. Assets are items they use to create value by selling products or services; liabilities show where and how the monies used to buy assets came from. Some assets and liabilities are short-term ones, while others are long-term ones. The phrase "short term" generally refers to a time period of less than one year.[1] Short-term assets are those that the firm consumes, sells, or replaces within a year. Likewise, short-term liabilities are those the firm expects to satisfy

---

[1]Some prefer to use the word "current" instead of the phrase "short term".

within a year. Long-term assets and liabilities pertain to time periods longer than a year. Working capital concerns short-term assets and liabilities.

Now let us identify short-term assets and liabilities. The most common short-term assets are the following:

- Cash;
- Accounts receivable — money owed by customers;
- Inventory — finished goods and goods in process;
- Short-term investments such as bank accounts; and
- Prepaid expenses.

Every company has short-term assets. Some companies may not have all the categories listed above, but no company can operate without most of the items on the list.

Short-term liabilities include the following items:

- Accounts payable — money owed to suppliers;
- Accrued wages — money owed to workers;
- Short-term debt — money owed to banks and other creditors; and
- Deferred taxes — money owed to the government.

Again, every company has short-term liabilities; most have all, or nearly all, the items in the list above.

Working capital is calculated by subtracting short-term liabilities from short-term assets, as seen in the formula below[2]:

$$\text{Working capital} = \text{Short-term assets} - \text{Short-term liabilities.} \quad (13.1)$$

Though it is not a hard and fast rule, working capital is generally greater than zero, meaning that short-term assets exceed short-term liabilities. Companies whose working capital is positive (i.e., their short-term assets exceed their short-term liabilities) are said to have "working capital". When short-term assets are less than short-term liabilities, the firm is described as having a "working capital deficit".

---

[2]Sometimes working capital is called "net working capital" or "net current assets". For simplicity, in this book we use the phrase "working capital".

Working capital management involves the administration of short-term assets and liabilities. The objective of working capital management is to monitor and maintain the company's accounts so that the firm has the necessary liquidity to be able to:

(1) repay maturing short-term indebtedness and
(2) pay vendor and employee bills as they come due,

while at the same time economizing on the amount of the firm's assets invested in short-term assets. Firms try to be as lean in their holdings of short-term assets as is prudent, given the flow of obligations requiring repayment. Simplistically, working capital management attempts to minimize working capital by reducing the firm's short-term assets (possibly with the exception of cash) and increasing its short-term liabilities (its sources of capital), while still maintaining an adequate level of liquidity.

Working capital provides the firm with operating liquidity. Without adequate working capital, the firm could not fund its daily operations. This means that suppliers would not be paid on time, employees would be told that their checks were being delayed, and banks and other creditors would not receive interest and principal repayment. Working capital provides the funds a company needs to redeem its short-term debt as it comes due and to pay for its operations as bills are presented. Without working capital, the firm fails. Its bankruptcy results from a default on its debts or from a failure to pay its bills. Even a profitable company that has poor working capital management policies may fail, since it may not be possible to convert its valuable assets into cash when funds are needed. The bulk of activities referred to as working capital management are concerned with monitoring and regulating the firm's inventories, accounts receivable, cash, accounts payable, and short-term debt.

Working capital management controls the flow of funds into and out of the firm. The speed and balance of the flow depend on working capital policies enacted by the firm. Figure 13.1 illustrates an active working capital management policy, and shows where funds come from and go to. As you review the figure, observe that each item is at least partially in the firm's control. That is, the firm can establish

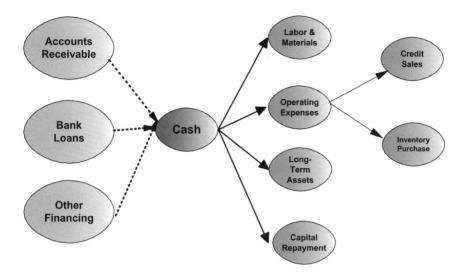

Fig. 13.1    Working Capital Flows.

policies that affect the size and rate of change in every item displayed in Fig. 13.1.

For example, the accounts receivable policy describes which customers are eligible to obtain financing from the firm and when that financing is to be repaid. The firm might give credit to buyers purchasing more than $1,000 of items, but require a cash payment from purchasers of smaller quantities. Similarly, the firm might require repayment in 10 days, or it could opt for a more lenient policy and allow repayment in 30 days. These decisions influence the amount of credit sales (seen on the far right-hand side of Fig. 13.1) and the timing of when these accounts receivable (seen on the far left-hand side of Fig. 13.1) convert into cash (seen in the middle of Fig. 13.1). Corporate policy decisions influence the dollar size and timing of changes in each circle in Fig. 13.1 in a manner similar to the accounts receivable discussion above.

Knowing what your working capital equals is a simple calculation; all you need to do is use equation (13.1). What is difficult is knowing when working capital is too high or too low. Several useful analytical tools have evolved over the years to help businesses gauge their working capital level. One tool is the cash conversion cycle. The material presented in the previous chapter on the cash conversion cycle is highly relevant to this discussion of working capital management. Readers may want to review that material. Basically, the cash conversion cycle measures how long it takes for a firm to turn raw materials back into cash. Firms with longer cash conversion cycles have worse working capital situations than similar companies with shorter cash conversion cycles. The three key parts of the cash conversion cycle calculation are accounts receivable, inventories, and accounts payable. Decisions to modify any one of the three affect the cash conversion cycle.

The cash conversion cycle has two components: the operating cycle and the payment deferral period.[3] The operating cycle includes both the average collection period (for accounts receivable) and the inventory conversion period. The operating cycle captures the time money is tied up in going from inventories to sales to accounts receivable to cash collection. The payment deferral period measures the length of time the firm can stretch its vendors before repaying them. The payment deferral period measures the time elapsing between the purchases of inventory and the repayment of vendors. The sum of the operating cycle and the payment deferral period equals the cash conversion cycle.

A second useful tool that companies use to control their working capital is a 13-week cash flow projection model. Such models help to maintain tight control over working capital over a short 13-week time frame. They are designed to capture the expected inflows and outflows of funds. A simplified 13-week cash flow model is presented in Table 13.1. The model shows that the firm has steady cash flow from operations, but has a scheduled repayment on its loan balance in week 11 and a compulsory tax payment due in week 12. As a consequence, its cash holdings are expected to be negative in weeks 12 and 13. Knowing in advance about the expected negative cash position allows the firm to rearrange its working capital and reduce its cash drains (it might, for example, reduce purchases for inventory starting

---

[3]See V.D. Richards and E.J. Laughlin, "A Cash Conversion Cycle Approach to Liquidity Analysis," *Financial Management*, Spring, 1980, pp. 32–38.

Table 13.1   13-Week Cash Flow Model.

| Week | 1 | 2 | 3 | 4 | 5 | 6 | 7 | 8 | 9 | 10 | 11 | 12 | 13 |
|---|---|---|---|---|---|---|---|---|---|---|---|---|---|
| Operating cash receipts | 10 | 10 | 10 | 10 | 10 | 10 | 10 | 10 | 10 | 10 | 10 | 10 | 10 |
| Payroll and benefits | 3 | 3 | 3 | 3 | 3 | 3 | 3 | 3 | 3 | 3 | 3 | 3 | 3 |
| Operating expenses | | | | | | | | | | | | | |
| Materials | 2 | 2 | 2 | 2 | 2 | 2 | 2 | 2 | 2 | 2 | 2 | 2 | 2 |
| Taxes | | | | | | | | | | | | 49 | |
| Utilities | 1 | 1 | 1 | 1 | 1 | 1 | 1 | 1 | 1 | 1 | 1 | 1 | 1 |
| Total outflow from operations | 6 | 6 | 6 | 6 | 6 | 6 | 6 | 6 | 6 | 6 | 6 | 55 | 6 |
| Net cash flow | 4 | 4 | 4 | 4 | 4 | 4 | 4 | 4 | 4 | 4 | 4 | −45 | 4 |
| Beginning cash | 1 | 5 | 9 | 13 | 17 | 21 | 25 | 29 | 33 | 37 | 41 | 35 | −10 |
| Loan balance | 30 | 30 | 30 | 30 | 30 | 30 | 30 | 30 | 30 | 30 | 30 | 20 | 20 |
| Loan payment | | | | | | | | | | | 10 | | |
| Cumulative cash | 5 | 9 | 13 | 17 | 21 | 25 | 29 | 33 | 37 | 41 | 35 | −10 | −6 |

in week 8 or 9) or possibly increase its cash inflows (for example, by reducing the amount of credit granted to customers). A 13-week cash flow model is not very sophisticated but, without one, firms are somewhat in the dark about the impact of their short-term obligations on their solvency and their cash position. Most turnaround consultants begin an assignment by calculating a 13-week cash flow model.

A third technique that companies follow to maintain control over their working capital is to monitor specific items that affect working capital. The list below contains several items that are typically watched for future working capital problems, and beside each item is how companies track the entry.

- Cash — 13-week cash flow model.
- Accounts receivable — monitoring of uncollectable accounts or average collection days.
- Inventories — monitoring of the level of inventories and the change in inventories.
- Bank loans — requests received from the bank for balance reductions or further information.

- Accounts payable — requests received from vendors for speedier payment or reduced credit lines.

A more scientific approach to monitoring working capital uses ratios. Perhaps the most popular of these ratios are as follows:

- Current ratio — short-term assets divided by short-term liabilities.
- Acid or quick ratio — short-term assets net of inventories divided by short-term liabilities.
- Cash flow-to-debt ratio — cash flow from operations divided by total debt.
- Ratio of working capital to total assets — working capital divided by total assets.
- Days sales outstanding — accounts receivable divided by daily credit sales.
- Ratio of cash plus marketable securities to short-term debt.

Each of these ratios is important as they target different items in the working capital accounts.

The advantage of ratios is that their unit values tend to be bounded. For example, a company's short-term assets and short-term liabilities might grow persistently, making it difficult to judge either's size. In contrast, the ratio of the two concepts (called the current ratio) is likely to remain within a bound of perhaps zero to 3.0.

Working capital decisions are short-term ones. Furthermore, most changes made that affect working capital are not permanent and can be reversed if required by circumstances. The usual method for evaluating the benefits of a working capital change is to determine how it would/might affect the firm's cash holdings. In some cases, such as a tightening in the accounts receivable policy, it may require a comparison between an increase in cash resulting from the change against a loss in profits due to customer response to the change.

Working capital management is related to the topic of sources and uses of funds, i.e., where funds are obtained from and where they are deployed. Though sources and uses of funds generally describe both long- and short-term decisions of the firm, it is also true that sources and uses can be viewed simply in the short term and used to assess working capital.

A helpful feature of sources and uses of funds is that they highlight the connection between items in a firm's working capital. At the highest level, a source brings working capital to the firm. But as an example of connectivity, a source is either a decrease in a short-term asset or an increase in a short-term liability. Similarly, a use consumes working capital. Another example of connectivity is how uses are either an increase in a short-term asset or a decrease in a short-term liability.

Sources and uses of funds can be confusing. For example, paying off a bank loan (a short-term liability) uses funds. What is confusing is that after paying off the loan the firm has more working capital (short-term assets minus short-term liabilities), but yet the firm has used up some of its funds. Similarly, an increase in inventory held by a firm increases its short-term assets and is a use of working capital. The confusion here is that working capital is higher, yet the firm has used some of its funds.

The confusion arises around sources and uses of funds because of the difference between stocks and flows. A stock variable is an aggregate amount calculated at a particular moment, like the size of the national debt. In contrast, a flow is the current amount measured over a period of time, like the national budget deficit. A higher budget deficit leads to a higher national debt, while a zero deficit leaves the debt unchanged. Applying this knowledge to working capital management and the sources and uses of funds helps to clear up the confusion: a firm's working capital (a stock) rises when it uses funds (the flow); the firm's working capital falls when it has a source of funds.

Working capital management applies the various sources and uses of funds available to the firm to ensure that supplies are bought, that workers' and debt obligations are paid, that adequate inventories are held, and that the firm collects the monies owed to it. Working capital management has a very short-term perspective focusing on short-term debts and near-term operational activities. Longer-term decisions such as capital budgeting decisions take a multi-year approach.

The basics of working capital management include a three-step process:

(1) Determine the necessary or appropriate level for each short-term asset and liability item.
(2) Identify the cost of exceeding or not reaching each item's necessary level, such as for inventory, notes payable, etc.
(3) Institute a program to reduce costs by changing the amount of a working capital component.

For example, with inventories, in step 1 a desired inventory level is established. In step 2, the firm determines the specific costs of holding too much inventory that arise from increasing the firm's investment in materials, work-in-progress, and finished goods; and the costs of having too little inventory, which inhibits the flow of production and idles other factors of production. Changes in busy activity, interest rates, and competition may alter the conclusions reached in steps 1 and 2, and may necessitate a further review. The third step is often the most difficult, since line managers may be reluctant to make changes. If the "lead with cash" culture is established within a firm, it is hoped that these natural hesitancies are forestalled before they materialize. With the new philosophy, managers realize that what is good for their unit is also good for the firm.

Fixing the appropriate level of accounts receivable to hold is a good example of how the "lead with cash" mentality is so important in working capital management. A firm's credit policy — which clients are offered credit and on what terms — affects sales and revenues by attracting or chasing away customers. Managers responsible for the sales department object to any policy other than one which is tolerant and provides credit regardless of creditworthiness. These managers personally benefit from reporting higher sales. However, sales that do not result in collections or which yield very slow collections have deleterious effects on cash flow and the cash conversion cycle. Credit managers thus opt for strict credit policies, since they do not want to have to chase customers for payment or report uncollectable accounts. Lax credit terms are not good; neither are overly strict terms. Managers need to come together and discuss the alternatives openly and honestly so that a credit policy which is best for the firm evolves.

*Lead with Cash* asserts, "Get over the balkanization of departments" and "find the right working capital policy for the firm, not just for the unit". It is important that corporate incentive policies accommodate the "lead with cash" culture by not penalizing managers who allow their units to take a hit for the good of the entire enterprise.

# 14. The Statement of Cash Flows: Six Red Flags*

When considering signs of financial distress that might lead to bankruptcy, most people know to look at the bottom line on the income statement: net income. A company that is in the red and reporting net losses rather than net income is of concern. While net losses do not by themselves indicate that a company is in financial distress, companies with net losses certainly deserve further investigation. Indeed, most of the companies we reviewed prior to the year in which they filed for bankruptcy reported net losses for all or most of the four years prior to filing.

We wondered what additional signs of financial distress we might find if we examined the cash flow statements of companies that later filed for bankruptcy. We obtained statements of cash flow from 20 publicly traded companies that filed for Chapter 11 bankruptcy protection between August 2008 and May 2009. The statement dates were for the fiscal year of or just prior to the filing date. Companies examined came from a variety of industries: airlines, computer equipment, consumer electronics, consumer products, entertainment, health and beauty products, paper and paper products, plastics, publishing, recreational vehicles, retail, software and IT services, and transportation components and equipment.

---

*This chapter was written by Julie H. Hertenstein and Marjorie B. Platt.

# Format of the Cash Flow Statement[1]

The cash flow statement is organized in three sections: operating activities, investing activities, and financing activities. Exhibit 14.1 presents an example of a simple cash flow statement.

Exhibit 14.1   Statement of Cash Flows (presented without numerical values).[2]

| | |
|---|---|
| **Cash Flow from Operating Activities** | |
| Net Income | xxx,xxx |
| Adjustments to reconcile net income to net cash provided by operating activities: | |
| Depreciation and amortization | xx,xxx |
| Changes in other accounts affecting operations: | |
| (Increase)/decrease in accounts receivable | x,xxx |
| (Increase)/decrease in inventories | x,xxx |
| (Increase)/decrease in prepaid expenses | x,xxx |
| Increase/(decrease) in accounts payable | x,xxx |
| Increase/(decrease) in taxes payable | x,xxx |
| Net cash provided by operating activities | xxx,xxx |
| | |
| **Cash Flow from Investing Activities** | |
| Capital expenditures | (xxx,xxx) |
| Proceeds from sales of equipment | xx,xxx |
| Proceeds from sales of investments | xx,xxx |
| Investment in subsidiary | (xxx,xxx) |
| Net cash provided by (used in) investing activities | (xxx,xxx) |
| | |
| **Cash Flow from Financing Activities** | |
| Payments of long-term debt | (xx,xxx) |
| Proceeds from issuance of long-term debt | xx,xxx |
| Proceeds from issuance of common stock | xxx,xxx |
| Dividends paid | (xx,xxx) |
| Purchase of treasury stock | (xx,xxx) |
| Net cash provided by (used in) financing activities | (xx,xxx) |
| | |
| **Increase (Decrease) in Cash** | **xx,xxx** |

---

[1]This section is excerpted from Julie H. Hertenstein and Sharon M. McKinnon, "Solving the Puzzle of the Cash Flow Statement," *Business Horizons*, Vol. 40, No. 1, 1997, pp. 69–76, which contains a broader discussion of the statement of cash flow beyond signs of financial distress.
[2]*Ibid.*, Figure 1.

*Cash flow from operating activities* shows the results of cash inflows and outflows related to the fundamental operations of the basic line or lines of business in which the company engages. For example, it includes cash receipts from the sale of goods or services, and cash outflows for purchasing inventory and paying rent and taxes. Nearly all companies choose the indirect format to present cash flows from operating activities. This approach assumes that most of the operating cash flows are already summarized in the net income figure, so it starts with that figure and makes an adjustment for everything that is not a true representation of "cash in and cash out" in net income.

The next section is called *cash flow from investing activities.* Here, you see the cash flows associated with purchases and sales of long-lived assets such as property, plant, and equipment, and purchases and sales of investments or subsidiaries.

The third section is called *cash flow from financing activities.* These are all the cash flows associated with financing the firm, including everything from selling and paying off bonds to issuing and repurchasing stock and paying dividends.

## Reviewing the Cash Flow Statement

We reviewed the cash flow statements of the 20 companies, and discovered red flags in each section. Of the six red flags we found, one was related to operating activities, two to investing activities, two to financing activities, and one to combined information from operating and investing activities. We will use cash flow statements from Sun-Times Media Group, Inc. (hereafter, "Sun-Times") to illustrate the red flags. Sun-Times filed for bankruptcy on March 31, 2009; Sun-Times' cash flow statements for the three years prior to filing for bankruptcy are shown in Exhibit 14.2. We will begin with the operating activities section of the cash flow statement, and work our way down the statement through investing activities and then financing activities.

Exhibit 14.2   Statement of Cash Flows for Sun-Times (2006–2008).[3]

## Consolidated Statement of Cash Flows for the Years Ended December 31 (in thousands of dollars)

| | 2008 | 2007 | 2006 |
|---|---|---|---|
| **Cash Flows from Operating Activities:** | | | |
| Net income (loss) | (353,499) | 271,630 | (56,673) |
| Income from discontinued operations | 0 | (1,599) | (20,957) |
| Income (loss) from continuing operations | (353,499) | 270,031 | (77,630) |
| Adjustments to reconcile income (loss) from continuing operations to net cash provided (used) in continuing operations: | | | |
| Depreciation and amortization | 26,665 | 32,074 | 33,878 |
| Deferred income taxes | 17,387 | 147,454 | 9,777 |
| Reduction of tax liabilities | (34,732) | (586,686) | |
| Other | 293,119 | 137,059 | (360) |
| Changes in current assets and liabilities (net): | | | |
| Accounts receivable | 9,547 | 3,715 | 18,338 |
| Inventories | 433 | 1,706 | 2,957 |
| Other current assets | 1,790 | 240 | (47,890) |
| Recoverable income taxes | 16,509 | 18,163 | (34,672) |
| Accounts payable and accrued expenses | (21,182) | (18,892) | (18,680) |
| Income taxes payable and other tax liabilities | (255) | 11,724 | 61,390 |
| Deferred revenue and other | (19,894) | (12,113) | (7,776) |
| *Cash provided by (used in) continuing operating activities* | *(64,112)* | *4,475* | *(60,668)* |
| **Cash Flows from Investing Activities:** | | | |
| Purchase of property, plant, and equipment | (16,475) | (11,645) | (9,134) |

(*Continued*)

---

[3]Based on information from Sun-Times' Annual Report, 2008.

Exhibit 14.2    (*Continued*)

|  | 2008 | 2007 | 2006 |
|---|---|---|---|
| Proceeds from sale of property, plant, and equipment | 3,522 | 4,808 | 231 |
| Investments, intangibles, and other non-current assets | (67) | (6,523) | (7,592) |
| Sale (purchase) of short-term investments, net | 0 |  | 57,650 |
| Purchase of investments | 0 | (48,200) | 0 |
| Proceeds on disposal of investments and other assets | 25,341 | 2,039 | 18,237 |
| Proceeds from sale of newspaper operations | 0 | 2,664 | 86,609 |
| Other | 138 | 8,830 | (266) |
| *Cash provided by (used in) investing activities* | *12,459* | *(48,027)* | *145,735* |
| **Cash Flows from Financing Activities:** |  |  |  |
| Repayment of debt and premium on debt extinguished | (38) | (6,976) | (1,193) |
| Net proceeds from issuance of equity securities | 0 | 0 | 9,851 |
| Repurchase of common stock | 0 | 0 | (95,744) |
| Dividends paid | 0 | 0 | (17,212) |
| Other | (8,234) | (2,320) | 2,150 |
| *Cash used in financing activities* | *(8,272)* | *(9,296)* | *(102,148)* |
| Net cash provided by (used in) discontinued operations | 0 | 0 | 6,756 |
| Effect of exchange rates on cash | (3,373) | 9,063 | (1,745) |
| Net increase (decrease) in cash and cash equivalents | (63,298) | (43,785) | (12,070) |
| Cash and cash equivalents at beginning of year | 142,533 | 186,318 | 198,388 |
| Cash and cash equivalents at end of year | 79,235 | 142,533 | 186,318 |

# Red Flag #1: Negative Net Cash Flow from Operating Activities

Net cash from operating activities is at the bottom line of the operating activities section; it summarizes all of the cash flows from the operating activities. Operating activities constitute the cash flow engine for a mature company.[4] In a healthy, mature company, the cash flow engine should generate enough cash to "keep the company whole" — that is, to replace the assets that have been used up in the course of the year, to pay the dividends, and hopefully to have a bit left over to allow the company to grow. The first red flag is negative net cash flow from operating activities.[5] Negative cash flow from operating activities means that, rather than generating cash to replace assets, pay dividends, and grow, operating activities are using more cash than they are generating, and so cash must be found elsewhere to make the company's products or provide its services. If you examine the cash flow statements for Sun-Times in Exhibit 14.2, you will see that it reported negative cash flow from operating activities in two of the three years prior to filing bankruptcy (2006 and 2008). The typical company we reviewed had negative cash flow from operating activities in two or three of the three years prior to filing bankruptcy. Some had negative cash flow from operating activities for most of the six years prior to filing bankruptcy.

# Red Flag #2: Cash Flow from Operating Activities Less than Capital Expenditures

Next, we move to the investing activities section and examine capital expenditures — the purchase of property, plant, and equipment. We will compare capital expenditures to net cash flow from operating activities (from the previous section). As stated earlier, the cash flow engine is expected to generate sufficient cash to purchase property, plant, and equipment.

---

[4]Hertenstein and McKinnon, *op. cit.*

[5]There are some situations in which negative cash flow from operating activities is normal; for example, for a start-up company. However, a start-up company will not normally show the other red flags discussed in this chapter.

Looking at Sun-Times' cash flow statements in 2006 and 2008, cash flow from operating activities was negative and obviously less than capital expenditures. However, even though cash flow from operating activities was positive in 2007, it was less than capital expenditures; it was not sufficient to purchase the property, plant, and equipment.

Furthermore, for most firms examined, in the three years prior to filing, even when cash flow from operating activities was positive, it was less than the capital expenditures for that year. Thus, despite the fact that the company might generate positive cash flows from operating activities in some years, it may not be generating sufficient cash to cover capital expenditures. We examined numerous firms where this problem was evident for most of the six years prior to filing.

## Red Flag #3: Capital Expenditures Less than Depreciation

As stated earlier, the cash flow engine should generate enough cash to "keep the company whole". But how much investment in capital expenditures is required to keep the company whole? Because nearly all companies use the indirect method to report cash flows from operating activities, depreciation expense is reported in the operating activities section as an adjustment to net income required to derive cash flows from operating activities.[6] Depreciation is an expense recorded to indicate the amount of the original cost of an asset that is used up each year over the lifetime of the asset. Thus, depreciation provides a very rough estimate of the amount of investment needed to "keep the company whole". In fact, depreciation most likely understates the amount needed to keep the company whole. Assets are depreciated based on their original cost; thus, because of inflation, the investment would have to be somewhat more than the depreciation amount to replace the used-up portion of the asset. Nonetheless, depreciation is a useful rough estimate. If a company

---

[6]This category is often labeled "depreciation and amortization". For most firms, depreciation expense constitutes most of this category. However, in interpreting this figure, the reader must consider the nature of the business and use judgment to estimate the depreciation amount.

invests somewhat more than depreciation in capital expenditures, it is likely keeping the company whole. If it invests considerably more than depreciation, the company is likely growing. If a company invests less than depreciation, then the company may be shrinking because it does not have sufficient cash to keep the company whole.

In Sun-Times' cash flow statements, "purchase of property, plant, and equipment" (capital expenditures) was considerably less than "depreciation and amortization" for each of the three years. In fact, for most of the companies we examined, capital expenditures were less than depreciation for all or most of the three years prior to filing; and for a number of companies, this pattern went back at least six years.

A company can acquire long-term assets in two ways: it can purchase the assets directly, or it can acquire them as part of the acquisition of another company. Hence, in deciding whether or not the company is spending enough to keep the company whole, one ought to also examine whether acquisitions were also made. Keep in mind that the amount paid for the acquisition is for the full bundle of assets, including current assets (such as receivables and inventory) as well as long-term assets (such as property, plant, and equipment).

## Red Flag #4: Decreasing Capital Expenditures

In a healthy company, capital expenditures required to keep the company whole would be expected to increase each year due to inflation. At Sun-Times, capital expenditures increased 27 percent from 2006 to 2007 and 41 percent from 2007 to 2008. However, in most other companies we examined, capital expenditures dropped significantly, especially in the three years prior to filing. This decline in capital expenditures suggests that the companies lacked sufficient cash to maintain capital investments at a healthy level.

For a few companies, not only were capital investments less than depreciation and declining, but the company also showed large proceeds from property, plant, and equipment sold or businesses divested, especially in the final year or two prior to filing. While most companies sell some property, plant, and equipment annually because it is outdated, worn out, or no longer needed, the amount of the proceeds is typically small, especially compared to capital expenditures. In a few of the firms we reviewed, the proceeds from sales of property, plant, and equipment exceeded the amount spent on property, plant, and equipment. Thus, when we examine the *net* cash flows for property, plant, and equipment, we may find that the firm is actually using property, plant, and equipment to generate cash, perhaps because it is so desperate for cash to fund its operations. At Sun-Times, the proceeds from the sale of property, plant, and equipment did not exceed the purchase of property, plant, and equipment; however, Sun-Times was generating a significant amount of cash by selling newspaper operations, especially in 2006.

## Red Flag #5: Declining or Eliminating Dividends

Next, we examine the financing activities section. In this section, the firm reports any dividends paid. Not all firms pay dividends. However, when a firm pays dividends, it is extremely reluctant to reduce the amount of dividends paid per share because of the significant and negative signal that this action sends to the stock market.[7] Hence, when total dividends paid declines significantly — or when dividends are eliminated — it is another sign that the company is desperate for cash. At Sun-Times, we can see that the dividends were paid in 2006, but were eliminated in 2007. Only five companies in the group of firms we examined paid dividends; of those, three reduced or eliminated them.

## Red Flag #6: Debt Repayment Exceeds Debt Proceeds

When a company shows several of the red flags discussed earlier, you may also want to examine the financing section to see whether the

---

[7]If the number of shares of stock outstanding declines (for example, due to a stock repurchase), there will likely be a decline in total dividends paid proportionate to the percentage of outstanding shares repurchased. Since this does not result from a reduction in dividends per share, the stock market would be less likely to view this as a negative signal.

proceeds from debt exceed debt repayment. In general, being a net repayer of debt might sound like a good thing; it suggests that you have enough cash available to pay down your debt and that you are becoming less dependent on lenders. However, in situations such as those described above — where operating activities are not generating cash and/or capital expenditures are not keeping the company whole and/or a company does not have enough cash to pay dividends — then, rather than having cash available to repay loans, it is more likely that the lenders are aware of the company's cash flow problems and do not want to loan more money to the company. Thus, being a net repayer in such situations results from the lenders' unwillingness to lend more to the company, combined with existing loans becoming due or being called.

Sun-Times did not borrow in the three years prior to filing, but did repay existing loans. Hence, debt repayment exceeded debt proceeds in each of the three years. At other companies we examined, there were numerous instances when debt repayment exceeded debt proceeds in some of the six years prior to filing.

## What's the Story?

Having examined the cash flow statement for each of the six red flags, we now need to examine the overall pattern of the red flags, combined with other knowledge about the company, to assess the degree of the company's financial distress. No single red flag is a definitive sign that the company will file for bankruptcy. In fact, we have indicated that in certain situations some red flags might be normal, as in the case of negative operating cash flows for a start-up company, while other red flags, like being a net repayer of debt, might actually be good news.

However, when several of these red flags occur repeatedly, then a dismal story emerges of a company unable to generate enough cash to keep itself whole, and being forced to undertake radical surgery by divesting assets and businesses in a desperate attempt to survive. In Table 14.1, we show the red flag patterns for Sun-Times and three other firms (Midway Games, Nortel, and Spectrum Brands) in the six

Table 14.1  Red Flag Patterns for Four Typical Bankrupt Companies.

| | Company | | | | | | | | | | | | | | | | | | | | | | | |
|---|---|---|---|---|---|---|---|---|---|---|---|---|---|---|---|---|---|---|---|---|---|---|---|---|
| | Sun-Times | | | | | | Midway Games | | | | | | Nortel | | | | | | Spectrum Brands | | | | | |
| Red Flag | '08 | '07 | '06 | '05 | '04 | '03 | '08 | '07 | '06 | '05 | '04 | '03 | '08 | '07 | '06 | '05 | '04 | '03 | '08 | '07 | '06 | '05 | '04 | '03 |
| (Net income) | X | X | X | X | | X | X | X | X | X | X | X | X | X | X | X | X | X | X | X | X | | | |
| #1 (CFO) | X | X | X | X | X | | X | X | X | X | X | X | X | X | X | X | X | X | X | X | X | | | |
| #2 CFO < cap. ex. | X | X | X | X | X | | X | X | X | X | X | X | X | X | X | X | X | X | X | X | X | | | |
| #3 Cap. ex. < D&A | X | X | X | X | | | X | X | X | X | | | X | X | X | | | | X | X | | X | | X |
| #4 Decreasing cap. ex. | | | X | X | | | X | X | | X | | | X | | | | | | X | X | X | | | |
| #5 Dividend payments[a] | * | E | R | D | D | D | * | * | * | * | * | * | * | * | * | * | * | * | * | * | * | * | * | * |
| #6 Net debt repayer | X | X | X | X | X | | | X | | | | | | | X | X | X | X | X | X | X | X | X | X |

*Note*: CFO, cash flow from operating (activities); cap. ex., capital expenditures; D&A, depreciation and amortization.
[a] D, dividends paid; R, reduced dividends paid; E, dividends eliminated; *, no dividends paid.

years before each company filed for bankruptcy. We also include net income in this table. Technically, net income is not a cash flow, and hence we have not included it among the red flags. However, as indicated in the beginning of this chapter, negative net income is often the first early warning signal noticed by observers; furthermore, net income is typically reported at the top of the cash flow statement due to firms' use of the indirect method to report cash flow from operating activities. For Sun-Times, and especially for Spectrum Brands, you can see that the red flags increased in the three years prior to filing. However, for Nortel and Midway Games, the red flags were evident for the full six years.

Although most of the companies we examined exhibited most or all of the red flags discussed above, not all did. In Table 14.2, we show the red flag patterns for two companies that filed for bankruptcy with cash flow statements *atypical* for the group examined (Gottschalks, Monaco Coach). Even these firms had some — albeit fewer — red flags.

## Summary

Statements of cash flow can be useful in assessing a company's financial condition. Our analysis of 20 companies which recently sought Chapter 11 bankruptcy protection indicated that all of them had at

Table 14.2   Red Flag Patterns for Two Atypical Bankrupt Companies.

| Red Flag | Company | | | | | | | | | | | |
| --- | --- | --- | --- | --- | --- | --- | --- | --- | --- | --- | --- | --- |
| | Gottschalks | | | | | | Monaco Coach | | | | | |
| | '08 | '07 | '06 | '05 | '04 | '03 | '07 | '06 | '05 | '04 | '03 | '02 |
| (Net income) | X | | | | | X | | | | | | |
| #1 (CFO) | | X | | | | | | | | X | | |
| #2 CFO < cap. ex. | | | | | | | | | | X | | X |
| #3 Cap. ex. < D&A | | | | | X | X | X | X | | | | |
| #4 Decreasing cap. ex. | X | X | | | X | | X | X | | X | | |
| #5 Dividend payments | * | * | * | * | * | * | D | D | D | D | * | * |
| #6 Net debt repayer | | | | X | X | X | X | X | | | X | |

least some weaknesses that were revealed in the cash flow statement. Knowing what to look for and how to interpret signs of distress early can help managers and investors understand the risks facing the firm. Early detection and action may be able to prevent further financial distress which may precede bankruptcy.

# 15. Cash Flow Details*

Among the most familiar formulas in finance is the one that describes how to calculate the present value of a project, a firm, or any stream of funds. The formula discounts future cash flows back to the present using an appropriate discount rate:

$$Present\,Value = \sum_{t=1}^{n} \frac{CashFlow_t}{(1+r)^t}, \qquad (15.1)$$

where

$CashFlow$ = net dollars received
$\quad t$ = time period
$\quad n$ = ending year for the firm or the project
$\quad r$ = discount rate.

Despite the formula's general acceptance, disagreements exist regarding its application. These disputes concern the calculation of cash flows, the construction of the terminal year, and the choice of discount rates. In addition, there is the question of whether the discount rate should change over time as the firm's financial policy changes. The first part of this chapter lays out these uncertainties in

*Originally published as Harlan D. Platt, "Cash Flow Contradistinctions". Reprinted with permission from *Commercial Lending Review*, March 2008. © 2008 CCH Incorporated. All rights reserved. Available at http://www. commerciallendingreview.com/. Valuable comments from Enrique Arzac, Dennis Lacey, Emery Trahan, and Thomas McCarthy improved the article.

greater detail. The remainder of the chapter presents a way to avoid re-estimating the discount rate each year.

## Measuring Cash Flow

Cash flow, the difference between money in and money out, was undoubtedly invented by the first merchant. As with anything ancient, numerous and conflicting definitions of cash flow have been developed by individuals with different needs. One way to understand alternate cash flow measurement techniques is to divide them into the two streams presented in Fig. 15.1. One stream values the firm's equity, while the other stream values the entire firm.

The version of cash flow familiar to most people combines net income plus depreciation and amortization. In Fig. 15.1, it is called simple cash flow (SCF). A common description of this cash flow measure is the sum of net income and non-cash charges:

Simple cash flow = Net income + Depreciation & Amortization.

$$(15.2)$$

SCF reflects the fact that the firm retains more than just net earnings, since income has been reduced by expenses that do not affect the firm's cash position.

The whole-firm straightforward cash flow concept is the well-known net operating profit after tax (NOPAT) measure. NOPAT's principal difference with SCF comes from its treatment of tax shields and interest and tax payments. NOPAT begins with unlevered net income (UNI), which is the net income that would accrue to the firm if its balance sheet had no interest-bearing obligations.

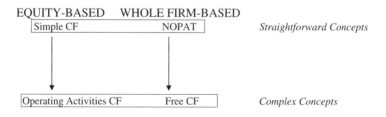

Fig. 15.1   Bifurcated Cash Flow Variations.

For a firm with interest-bearing debt, UNI is greater than net income.

$$\text{Unlevered net income} = \text{Net income} + (1 - \text{Tax rate})$$

$$\times (\text{Interest expense} - \text{Interest income}).^{1}$$

$$(15.3)$$

Essentially, UNI adds back to net income the interest paid by the firm, while subtracting out the tax shield that the firm gained from deducting interest payments. In other words, UNI reflects returns to both equity and debt holders and measures the return to the firm. Adding the change in deferred taxes to UNI creates NOPAT. Deferred taxes arise because some taxes reported on the firm's income statement are not actually paid in the current period. Tax discrepancies reflect differences in depreciation charges between financial statements and tax statements. Deferred taxes appear on the firm's balance sheet as a long-term liability. NOPAT equals UNI plus the change in deferred taxes:

$$\text{NOPAT} = \text{UNI} + \Delta \text{deferred taxes}, \qquad (15.4)$$

where $\Delta$ indicates a change in value between two time periods.

The difference between SCF and NOPAT arises because NOPAT measures the returns to the entire firm, while SCF reports cash flow to equity.

As seen in Fig. 15.1, other more complex cash flow measures have been developed. These are better-known concepts than either SCF or NOPAT. Operating activities cash flow (OACF)[2] extends SCF, while free cash flow (FCF) does the same for NOPAT. The complex cash flow measures (OACF and FCF) include additional sources of cash flow that are not part of the straightforward formulas.[3] For the most part, these additional items are changes in net working capital

---

[1]One can find UNI = net income + net interest expense after tax = $(1 - \text{tax rate})$ EBIT (earnings before interest and taxes).

[2]OACF is included in the statement of cash flows.

[3]Do not confuse OACF with operating cash flow, which equals EBIT + depreciation $-$ taxes.

(accounts receivable, inventories, prepaid expenses, accounts payable, and taxes payable). OACF starts with net income plus depreciation (SCF), and then includes changes in net working capital[4]:

$$\text{OACF} = \text{SCF} - \Delta \text{ net working capital.} \tag{15.5}$$

Similarly, FCF begins with NOPAT, but then adds back depreciation and subtracts capital expenditures and changes in net working capital (NOPAT already includes changes in deferred taxes, so this part of changes in working capital is not included)[5]:

$$\text{FCF} = \text{NOPAT} + \text{Depreciation} - \text{CAPEX}$$

$$- \Delta \text{ net working capital.} \tag{15.6}$$

Table 15.1 helps differentiate between the four concepts.

Table 15.1    Four Flavors of Cash Flow.

|  | Simple — Equity | Complex — Equity | Simple — Whole Firm | Complex — Whole Firm |
|---|---|---|---|---|
|  | SCF | OACF | NOPAT | FCF |
| Net income | • | • | • | • |
| Depreciation | • | • |  | • |
| Net interest less tax benefit |  |  | • | • |
| Capital expenditures |  |  |  | • |
| Δ deferred taxes |  | • | • | • |
| Δ accounts receivable |  | • |  | • |
| Δ inventories |  | • |  | • |
| Δ prepaid expenses |  | • |  | • |
| Δ accounts payable |  | • |  | • |

• denotes included items.

---

[4]Δ net working capital is the difference between current assets and current liabilities, with both the changes in cash and short-term debt removed by subtracting out the increase in cash and adding back the increase in debt. See Enrique Arzac, *Valuation for Mergers, Buyouts, and Restructuring*, John Wiley & Sons, Inc., Hoboken, NJ, 2005.
[5]Some analysts prefer maintenance CAPEX, which just allocates sufficient dollars to allow the firm to remain at its current level.

Obviously, no single cash flow measure is correct. Complex measures such as OACF and FCF are more comprehensive than the others, so it can be said that they more fully reflect the firm's total cash flow. Yet surprisingly, SCF is the cash flow measure with the most predictive power when researchers attempt to predict cash flow from operations one or two periods ahead.[6] Straightforward cash flow concepts such as SCF or NOPAT also have the advantage of being easy to calculate, describe, understand, and track.

Changes in working capital that are added to the simple measures of cash flow are called accruals. By including accrual accounts, complex cash flow measures note how much a company owes to others and what cash revenues it can anticipate. However, accrual changes may be impermanent consequences of soon-to-be-reversed transactions that will be reflected in the next period's cash flow. If so, this period's accrual changes to cash flow may not be very informative.

In deciding which form of cash flow to use, start by asking whether you need cash flows available to equity holders or those available to the entire firm. The primary difference is whether one is valuing common shares or the entire enterprise. In the former case, one might be considering buying a company's stock; while in the latter case, the analysis might be whether to buy the entire firm. Loan officers, of course, need to value the entire firm. If the need is for an equity valuation, start with SCF and progress to OACF if more details are desired. When valuing the firm, do the same with NOPAT and FCF; start with a simple cash flow measure and move to a more complex measure as necessary.

A useful way to view differences between the four measures of cash flow discussed above is by example. In Table 15.2, cash flows for the fiscal year 2006 for Exxon Mobil Corporation (Exxon) are presented for each of the four measures. Exxon's cash flows range between US\$37 billion and US\$52 billion, depending upon which cash flow measure is applied — a more-than-40-percent difference in cash

[6]See Robert M. Bowen, David Burgstahler, and Lane A. Daley, "Evidence on the Relationships Between Earnings and Various Measures of Cash Flow," *The Accounting Review*, Vol. 61, No. 4, 1986, pp. 713–725.

Table 15.2    Exxon Mobil Corporation Cash Flows for 2006 (in millions of USD).

|  | SCF | OACF | NOPAT | FCF |
|---|---|---|---|---|
| Net income | $39,500 | $39,500 | $39,500 | $39,500 |
| Depreciation | 11,416 | 11,416 |  | 11,416 |
| Net interest less tax benefit |  |  | 425.1 | 425.1 |
| Capital expenditures |  |  |  | (15,462) |
| Δ deferred taxes |  | 1,717 | 1,717 | 1,717 |
| Δ accounts receivable |  | −181 |  | −181 |
| Δ inventories |  | −1,057 |  | −1,057 |
| Δ prepaid expenses |  | −385 |  | −385 |
| Δ accounts payable |  | 1,160 |  | 1,160 |
| **Cash Flow** | **$50,916** | **$52,170** | **$41,642** | **$37,133** |

flow. Exxon is virtually a debt-free company. Thus, adding back net interest less tax benefits does little to enhance the value of Exxon. As a consequence, the lowest cash flow value is FCF, which is the complex cash flow measure of firm value. Of course, FCF is also the only cash flow measure to include capital expenditures less depreciation. OACF reports the largest cash flow value primarily because it includes depreciation and excludes capital expenditures. Again, it is hard to say based simply on the calculated values which cash flow measure is correct or the best. However, at least the choice is there.

## The Terminal Year

Sometimes it is not practical to extend the cash flow forecast out to the firm's final year. In the case of Exxon, the final year may be centuries from now. Instead, it is common to end the forecast period after a fixed number of years (10 years, for example) and then determine a terminal value for years beyond the forecast period. This alters the basic present-value formula slightly:

$$PresentValue = \sum_{t=1}^{n} \frac{CashFlow_t}{(1+r)^t} + \frac{TV}{(1+r)^n}, \qquad (15.7)$$

where

$TV$ = terminal-year value.

$TV$ is typically calculated by applying a future growth rate estimate to the cash flow forecast for the final year:

$$TV = \frac{CashFlow_N(1+g)}{(DiscountRate - g)}, \qquad (15.8)$$

where

$g$ = assumed growth rate in cash flow for years beyond $N$.

A common problem encountered in calculating $TV$ occurs when $g$ is greater than the discount rate. In that case, the formula produces a negative nonsense value. This issue is generally resolved by assuming that the rapidly growing firm's permanent growth rate declines toward the mean of all firms' long-term growth rates.

A bigger issue often overlooked in $TV$ calculations is the essential need for $TV$ to be derived in a steady-state year. The firm is in a long-term steady state when future capital expenditure needs are exactly met by future depreciation. In other words, the steady-state firm is self-sustaining. It no longer requires net capital expenditures or net working capital investment. If the firm is not in a steady state, then future cash flows would be lower whenever a major investment cycle began in the future. In that case, the analyst must adjust the estimate of future cash flow downward by subtracting additional capital expenditure and working capital investments.

A final conundrum concerns the calculation of the future growth rate, $g$. The analyst begins by estimating revenue, costs, and cash flow in the long run. This work takes account of macroeconomic, industry, technology, and market share forecasts. Comparing future growth rate estimates to historical growth rates helps evaluate the forecast's reasonableness.[7] Another approach sets $g$ equal to a reasonable fraction (e.g., 80 percent) of the firm's recent (e.g., five-year) actual growth rate. But this still leaves unanswered whether the

---

[7] Enrique Arzac illustrates this point well in his book, *Valuation for Mergers, Buyouts, and Restructuring, op. cit.*

Table 15.3    Hypothetical Firm with Volatile Growth Rate.

|  | 5 Years Ago | 4 Years Ago | 3 Years Ago | 2 Years Ago | 1 Year Ago |
|---|---|---|---|---|---|
| Cash flow | $1.00 | $1.10 | $1.21 | $1.33 | $1.00 |
| Annual growth |  | 10% | 10% | 10% | (25%) |
| Growth factor |  | 1.1 | 1.1 | 1.1 | 0.75 |

growth rate is calculated as a geometric or an arithmetic average. While this may sound trivial, it is in fact an important empirical question.[8]

Consider a hypothetical firm's growth path of cash flow in Table 15.3. This example purposely has the firm growing at a steady 10-percent annual rate and then declining by 25 percent in the last year so that the firm ends up with the same cash flow in the last year as it had in the first year. Two possibilities are available for estimates of $g$ with this data:

- The estimate of $g$ is the arithmetic average of the growth factors, i.e., 1.25 percent.
- The estimate of $g$ is the geometric average of the growth factors, i.e., 0.00 percent.

The two methods derive different estimates of the future growth rate. Which one is correct? Some might argue that the use of the arithmetic average is correct because it gives equal weight to all the years. That is, it mixes the years with 10-percent growth together with the one year with negative 25-percent growth to arrive at the 1.25-percent estimate. Proponents of the geometric mean method argue instead that if the firm has not increased cash flow over the five years, then it is not reasonable to assume that cash flow will grow in the future, and they use a 0-percent future growth rate. Again, the analyst must choose.

---

[8] I want to thank Anand Venkateswaran for bringing this interesting issue to my attention.

## The Discount Rate

The most commonly used discount rate is the weighted average cost of capital (WACC). WACC is calculated as the linear combination of the after-tax cost of equity and debt, each weighted by their proportional shares of the firm's capital structure[9]:

$$WACC = \left(\frac{E}{V} \times k^e\right) + \left[\frac{D}{V} \times k^d \times (1 - T)\right],  \qquad (15.9)$$

where

$k^e$ = cost of equity
$k^d$ = cost of debt
$E$ = market value of equity
$D$ = market value of debt
$V = E + D$
$T$ = tax rate.

So where is the controversy here? Everything looks fairly straightforward and everyone is familiar with the formula. Actually, there are numerous issues. Simple questions include these:

- Does debt equal short- plus long-term debt or the difference between total assets and total equity? Not using the former can lead to error and confusion.
- Is the tax rate set at the statutory tax rate or the effective rate? Generally, the statutory rate is used.
- How is $k^d$ measured? Dollars of interest paid over debt is the measure.
- What if the firm is private? Book values are generally used.
- Do preferred shares belong in equity or debt? They are given their own category and weights, taking into account whether their dividend is tax-deductible trust-preferred or not.

One difficult question remains: how do you measure $k^e$? Textbooks present this well-known formula derived from the capital asset pricing

---

[9]Some companies then add a premium to WACC and use this higher rate as the internal hurdle, thereby pushing business units to seek more profitable transactions.

model:

$$k^e = k_f + (ERP \times \beta), \tag{15.10}$$

where

$k^e =$ cost of equity
$k_f =$ cost of riskless debt
$ERP =$ equity risk premium
$\beta =$ the firm's beta.

Again, all of this seems easy enough, but questions arise:

- How do you measure $k_f$? Generally, the 10-year Treasury is used.
- What is the value of $ERP$? Estimates range from near 0 to 8 percent for public companies; private company ERPs may be substantially higher.
- How do you calculate $\beta$? A 60-month regression is generally run.
- Is $k^e$ the same for large and small firms? A size premium is often added for small firms.

Providing answers to these questions allows one to calculate WACC.

Now consider what happens if the firm's financial condition changes over time. Suppose that the cost of equity and debt remain constant but the firm retains a growing share of its net income, causing the equity share of its capital structure to grow (Table 15.4). As a result of the changing capital structure, the firm's WACC increases over time from 8.4 percent to 8.8 percent. The analyst must therefore recalculate WACC each year for every company being reviewed. This is a tedious process.

Table 15.4    Effect of Increasing Equity on WACC.

|  | Year 1 | Year 2 | Year 3 |
| --- | --- | --- | --- |
| Equity share | 0.40 | 0.43 | 0.46 |
| Debt share | 0.60 | 0.57 | 0.54 |
| $k^e$ | 0.12 | 0.12 | 0.12 |
| $k^d \times (1 - T)$ | 0.06 | 0.06 | 0.06 |
| WACC | 0.084 | 0.086 | 0.088 |

## Avoiding Changing WACC over Time

A simpler approach called the compressed adjusted present value (CAPV) method may be an alternative. The CAPV method avoids the task of making repeated WACC calculations. The solution that CAPV relies upon is to put the tax shield from debt into the cash flows, and then it removes the tax shield (as seen in equation (15.9)) from the discount rate calculation. There are two steps to this process. First, capital cash flows are determined.[10] Capital cash flows are simply FCF plus the tax shield from debt (which had been removed before net interest was added in):

$$\text{Capital cash flow} = \text{FCF} + \text{Tax shield}. \qquad (15.11)$$

Second, to balance the placement of the tax shield into cash flows (capital cash flow), the discount rate is recalculated as the cost of the unlevered firm, $k^u$:

$$k^u = k_f + \left(1 + \frac{D}{E}\right)^{-1} \times \beta \times ERP, \qquad (15.12)$$

where

$$\left(1 + \frac{D}{E}\right)^{-1} \times \beta = \beta^A = \text{the asset beta.}$$

The difference between the asset and equity betas is that the former reflects the risk of the entire firm, while the latter reflects the risk of the firm's equity. But the difference between $k^u$ and *WACC* is more than the fact that they rely on different betas. *WACC*, which includes the tax shield, must be recalculated each year; while $k^u$, which does not include the tax shield, needs to only be calculated once.

The formula for determining present value follows:

$$PresentValue = \sum_{t=1}^{n} \frac{CashFlow_t}{(1 + k^u)^t} + \frac{TV}{(1 + k^u)^n}. \qquad (15.13)$$

---

[10]Capital cash flow terminology comes from Richard Ruback, "Capital Cash Flows: A Simple Approach to Valuing Risky Cash Flows," *Financial Management*, Vol. 31, 2002, pp. 85–103.

With the CAPV simplification, present value is determined by estimating multi-year cash flows, one $k^u$, and one $TV$.

## Conclusion

While the set of choices for measuring cash flow may appear to be intertwined and complicated, in fact the task is not that difficult. The analyst starts by determining whether information is needed on the value of the firm or its equity. Then, he or she evaluates whether they can resolve their need with a simple cash flow measure or whether they require a complex answer. Loan officers generally need to evaluate cash flows for a firm. In some cases, the loan analyst may wish to determine both simple and complex cash flow values and to treat the answer more as a band than as a point estimate.

PART III

# 16. Reflections from Turnaround and Crisis Managers

## A. Michael F. Gries and Michael P. Healy — Working Capital: How It Influences Cash Flow

### Introduction

Over the past 25 years, the U.S. and global economies have experienced robust growth, and credit markets and products have grown with them. Corporate treasurers and chief financial officers have grown accustomed to this easy credit. However, with the recent downturn in the economy, companies are experiencing declining revenues coupled with restricted access to credit. Capital markets have experienced a severe "flight to safety", and many banks no longer have the ability to extend new or additional credit to companies. Almost every sector of the economy has retrenched, and firms are shoring up their balance sheets before looking to expand. This is evidenced in the aggregate amount of cash and cash equivalents being held by the companies in the S&P 500 index (excluding those in the financial sector), which ballooned to US$561 billion at the end of FY08 from US$199 billion in FY00, a 182-percent increase.[1] As a result of these events, firms are quickly realizing not only the importance of cash, but how cash is used in their operations (i.e., working capital). In order to fully understand cash, a firm needs to understand its

---

[1] Data from Capital IQ. Data based upon S&P 500 companies, excluding those in the financial sector, as of April 29, 2009.

working capital demands. The typical firm in the S&P 500 has only 18 percent of its total current assets in cash and cash equivalents; while accounts receivable and inventory, two large components of working capital, account for approximately 44 percent.[2] With vendors stretching payables to manage their own cash and customers having their capacity constricted, the management of working capital is becoming critical to the survival of many businesses.

While many firms have a treasury department dedicated to monitoring bank accounts and the associated cash transactions, very few of these are tasked with monitoring or analyzing working capital. In normal times, working capital management is often overlooked as market forces tend to balance the growth of its components and credit is easily accessible to mitigate any temporary imbalances. In turbulent times, firms can quickly find themselves with insufficient cash balances and limited access to capital. Unfortunately, many firms realize the importance of working capital management too late and suffer severe consequences as a result.

### Overview of Working Capital and Its Components

As has been said many times, working capital is the lifeblood of all firms, and is affected directly and indirectly by almost every aspect of business. Specifically, it is the capital that is being used by a business at any point in time to fund current assets and run the day-to-day operations.[3] A firm cannot function without working capital and, if mismanaged, can severely hamper both the growth and profitability of a business or even be a significant contributor to its demise. Companies too often do not consider the impact of a business decision on working capital until it presents a problem. Working capital is the "oil" in a business' economic engine: too little and the business stalls; too much and the business cannot run at maximum efficiency

---

[2]Data from Capital IQ. Data based upon S&P 500 companies as of April 21, 2009.

[3]Eugene F. Brigham, *Financial Management Theory*, 9th ed., Harcourt Brace College Publishers, Fort Worth, TX, 1999, p. 792.

or profitability. The most common components of working capital include the following.

*Cash*

Cash is the simplest form of working capital and usually represents the starting point in the cash conversion cycle. Cash is the most flexible component of working capital in that it can be quickly converted into other forms such as inventory, accounts receivable, or accounts payable. It is the only component of working capital that can be converted into more permanent capital as well as to fund strategic initiatives. Cash, however, rarely generates meaningful economic returns to shareholders, and therefore maintaining too much cash can dampen or inhibit the growth and profitability of a business. By comparison, too little cash and a business may not be able to react to unplanned events (economic slowdowns, strikes, or natural disasters), maintain credit ratings, or capitalize on opportunities like trade discounts or strategic acquisitions.

*Cash Equivalents (Marketable Securities)*

Cash equivalents are monies held in short-term (less than one year), highly liquid investments. In order to qualify as a cash equivalent, it is important that the investment be able to be converted into cash quickly and without a discount. In most cases, cash equivalents are created when a firm has excess cash which it wishes to retain for the reasons mentioned above, but wants to increase returns with limited risk. Examples of short-term securities include:

- Treasury bills;
- Commercial paper;
- Certificates of deposit; and
- Repurchase agreements (overnight and term).

*Accounts Receivable*

Accounts receivable (A/R) is money that is owed to a business usually as a result of the business extending credit to its customers in the ordinary course. A/R most often varies with sales, and terms are often changed to attract new customers and increase sales with existing customers. While the creation of A/R is nearly inevitable, it has to be balanced against its use of cash when being offered. Firms often do not look at A/R as an expense or use of cash because no monies are transferred; however, growth in A/R is very much a cash expense in terms of the cash conversion cycle. In times of rapid expansion, a highly successful firm can literally grow itself out of business. This was the fate of many start-ups during the dot-com boom in the late 1990s. As business boomed, firms poured money into expanding manufacturing operations, inventory, and the associated back office support. As these investments often did not produce salable product for several months and were sold on terms creating receivables, many firms ran out of cash in the middle of a large expansion, causing them to miss production deadlines or be unable to fulfill orders.

*Inventory*

Inventory consists of the goods or services that a firm uses to create its product. Depending upon the type of business, inventory can consist of physical material (for manufacturing firms) or financial products (for financial service firms). In manufacturing companies, inventory can reside in many different forms: (1) raw materials, (2) supplies, (3) work in progress, and (4) finished goods. Inventory is usually created through the purchase of goods (real or financial, depending upon the type of business).

## Overview of the Cash Conversion Cycle

The cash conversion cycle is the cycle through which a company's capital moves as it is converted into different forms of working capital. The cycle helps a company identify how much capital is allocated to each component of the cycle at any one time, and the length of time between the payment of what a business owes (or its accounts payable) and the collection of what a business is owed (or its accounts receivable). Understanding both the amount of working capital in the cycle and the length of the cycle is important because the cash invested in each form is otherwise unavailable to the business during that time period. Active management of investment levels in working capital is a key characteristic of successful companies.

The five basic components of the cycle are detailed below:

- Cash — Cash on hand (initial equity, debt, or previously earned profits).
- Inventory purchases — Converted into products or services (accounts payable may be created if the supplier extends credit to the firm).
- Production expense — Labor and overhead costs will be incurred to convert the inventory into finished goods and services (accrued expenses are created over various lengths of time).
- Sale of goods and services — Accounts receivable may be created if the business extends credit to buyers.
- Ending cash balance — In a profitable firm, ending cash will be higher than starting cash if accounts payable and accounts receivable are properly managed and the company is not overleveraged.[4]

As detailed above, the level and term of any payable or receivable created during the cycle plays a pivotal role in managing cash balances.

When trying to optimize the cash conversion cycle, the goal of a firm should be to minimize the amount of cash that is used or "trapped" in the cycle without hampering profitability or growth. Figure 16.1 shows an example of a typical cash conversion cycle.

In order to minimize the amount of cash that is used or tied up in the cash conversion cycle and maximize economic returns, a company needs to balance its payables and accruals related to purchasing with its receivables related to sales and profitability. Specifically, companies must strive to minimize the time between when cash is used to purchase goods and services and when cash is received from the sale of product related to those goods and services. The ability of a firm

---

[4]Overleveraged means a balance sheet condition in which a firm is unable to service its debt load with future sustainable cash flows and available capital sources.

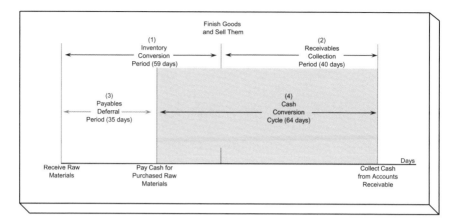

Fig. 16.1   A Typical Cash Conversion Cycle.[5]

to reduce this window of time is a function of internal management, the industry in which the company operates, its relative size, and its degree of profitability. Ideally, cash from the sale of goods and services would be received at the same time that payment for the goods and services used to make the end product is due, eliminating the need to tie up any cash or rely on outside financing. Some businesses are actually able to reduce this window to zero or even negative days, which allows them to finance their operations entirely through third-party capital, which has no net cost to the firm.[6] Companies use several techniques to minimize the length of time capital is used in order to reduce the amount of working capital needed for operations. Common ways to reduce the window of time in the cycle include the following:

• Increase both the percentage of purchases that receive credit terms and the credit terms themselves (payables). Both of these actions will create cash availability.

---

[5]Eugene F. Brigham, *op. cit.*, p. 870.

[6]In this situation, the firm is not required to use any of its capital to fund payables and as such does not sacrifice any potential earnings from the reinvestment of that capital.

- Decrease both the percentage of sales on credit and the credit terms themselves (receivables). Both of these actions will shorten the cash conversion cycle and increase available cash.
- Reduce the amount of on-hand inventory. Excess inventory is only economically practical when the cost of inventory is expected to rise at a rate, less what can be passed on to customers, that exceeds the cost of capital. This rarely happens over long periods of time and usually only happens to firms whose products have high elasticity.
- Offer vendors and suppliers discounts if they remit payment within a specified number of days. Common discounted terms include a 2-percent discount if payment is received within 10 days or full payment in 30 days.
- Sell receivables to third parties at a discount. This has the dual effect of immediately freeing up cash and removing the risk associated with non-payment by a vendor or supplier. However, if the discount is too large, it can eliminate any benefits.

## Net Working Capital

While working capital looks at the aggregate amount of capital being tied up in current assets at any point in time, net working capital looks at the available or "free" capital at any point in time. Specifically, net working capital is the difference between a firm's current assets and its current liabilities.[7] When evaluating working capital, firms usually look at net working capital to account for all aspects of the cash conversion cycle. The primary components of current liabilities that are used in calculating net working capital include the following.

### Accounts Payable

Accounts payable (A/P) is money that a firm owes to third-party vendors, usually as a result of the vendor extending credit to the company for purchases of goods and services. A/P can be thought

---

[7]Eugene F. Brigham, *op. cit.*, p. 792.

of as the inverse of A/R. Like A/R, firms often do not look at A/P as a source of cash because no monies actually flow to the company when a payable is created, but growth in A/P delays a cash use in the cash conversion cycle.

*Accrued Expenses*

Accrued expenses are created due to timing differences between when liabilities (other than for the purchase of goods or services that goes into the cost of inventory and is invoiced at the time the purchase is made) are incurred and either invoiced or paid. They are similar to A/P, but generally relate to expenses that are generally not evidenced by anything tangible (like a widget or an invoice). Examples include employee payroll, Social Security, or income taxes due to government agencies, and sales tax collected by a business but not yet due to be paid. A business generally has the use of monies associated with the expenses accrued until payments are made. As there is almost always no cost of this form of working capital (such as interest expense), the company receives short-term financing at no cost. In addition, accruals generally increase as business activities rise, creating an automatic source of working capital which hopefully grows in relative proportion to the business' needs. However, since the terms and conditions of accruals are dependent upon contractual agreements, companies have little control over managing the level of this type of credit unless they are willing and able to change suppliers.

## Other Types of Working Capital

Companies can supplement their cash position through the use of alternate forms of working capital. Companies may elect to raise additional cash to expand operations, refinance debt obligations, or acquire other firms. Common alternative sources of cash include:

- Bank term loans;
- Public or private (non-bank) debt offerings;
- Public or private equity sales; and
- Revolving lines of credit.

While all of the above serve to increase a firm's cash position, bank loans and debt and equity offerings usually require a significant amount of preparation and, in the case of raising equity, may take up to a year. As such, they are almost always reserved for longer-term strategic projects and should not be relied upon to meet the daily cash requirements of a business. Revolving lines of credit, depending upon the size of the commitment, vary in the length of time they take to place. However, lines of credit are usually put in place to supplement cash availability when the working capital needs of the firm absorb too much of a firm's capital. Firms can also look to monetize assets that they own as a way to convert "value" into cash in order to supplement their working capital position. Common examples of this include sale leaseback transactions on owned real estate (corporate headquarters, distribution facilities, warehouses, etc.) and long-term investments in other companies or assets (ownership stakes in spin-offs, investments in private corporations, etc.). While all investments need to be reviewed from time to time and realized when market conditions are opportune, these types of transactions should not be considered when planning or managing the day-to-day operations of a firm. Realizations of these types of assets to fund daily operations are almost always an early warning sign of underlying liquidity problems within a company.

### *Accounting Profits vs. Cash Profits*

Earnings (as defined by accounting profits or net income) and cash profits, although related, are two very different measurements of a firm's profitability or loss. Net income and the related earnings are created by accounting conventions and include non-cash items such as depreciation and amortization (D&A). Net income, as governed in the United States by the Generally Accepted Accounting Principles (GAAP), attempts to calculate the accounting profitability of a firm during a specific period of time. Cash profits or losses, on the other hand, look only at the changes in cash receipts and disbursements during a specific period of time. On a stand-alone basis, neither accounting profits nor cash profits can be relied upon to accurately measure a business' performance. However, observers too often become focused on accounting profits and lose sight of cash. Earnings before interest, taxes, depreciation, and amortization (EBITDA) — a non-GAAP financial metric — is often used as a proxy for free cash flow as it can be quickly derived from a GAAP set of financials. However, it is necessary to understand other income statement items in order to fully understand cash flow management. For example, while EBITDA excludes depreciation and amortization, which are accounting conventions for capturing the cost of an asset over its useful life and as such affect net income, it also excludes interest and tax expenses, which are often cash expenses. Other items that can affect cash flow but not GAAP earnings include prepaid items such as advertising, benefits, supplies, taxes, insurance, and maintenance. While these are all cash expenses, they are often charged against earnings in subsequent periods to align economic expenses with use. As a result, accounting profits can be a poor proxy for measuring cash flows, and should not be used to manage or budget cash flow.

## Working Capital Management

Working capital management refers to decisions related to the types and amounts of current assets and the means of financing them, including:

- Levels of cash and inventories;
- Credit and collection policies surrounding A/R;
- Negotiations with suppliers over A/P terms;
- Short-term borrowing and alternative financing opportunities;
- Inventory financing; and
- Receivables financing.

Working capital management is generally concerned with the day-to-day operations rather than long-term business decisions. Additionally, working capital decisions are most often made in response to strategic decisions. For example, if a company was planning to introduce a new product or open a new location, part of the planning process would examine how the project would be financed. The company would review its working capital position and determine how much, if any, additional financing would be required. As a result, working capital management policies target short-term concerns such as:

- Availability of raw material and inventories;
- Maintenance of required operational levels;
- Taking advantage of credit purchases and discounts; and
- Daily cash account balances.

As the average firm has approximately 40 percent[8] of its capital tied up in current assets, decisions regarding working capital are of great importance to business success and should be viewed with a more strategic thought process (i.e., supply chain in the automotive industry). This is especially true for smaller companies which have less access to the capital markets and, as such, a limited number of financing options. This requires them to rely upon creating their own credit through accounts payable, and bank loans and credit secured by inventories and/or accounts receivable. In addition, small firms typically lease a larger proportion of their fixed assets to avoid large, one-time expenses, but cannot avoid investments in inventory, cash, and receivables.

While the goal of minimizing working capital is admirable, it is important to remember that there is almost always a direct correlation between sales growth and the level of current assets. When demand for a company's products or services increases, the increase must be met with additional supply. As a result, production volumes need to rise to meet that supply/demand imbalance. Higher production, however, requires greater investment in inventories and personnel. Additionally, if a firm buys inventory on credit, its accounts payable increase; and when it sells on credit, its accounts receivable

---

[8]Mike Reynolds, *Financial Management Theory*, 4th ed., Harcourt Brace College Publishers, San Diego, CA, 1985, p. 731.

increase. Higher sales therefore require larger investments in work-ing capital, which comes either from existing capital or from new financing. So long as the product is profitable, the strategic deci-sion to increase production is easy. However, during the growth or expansion phase of production, balances within the stages of the cash conversion cycle can become unbalanced. For example, large amounts of inventory may need to be bought well before any proceeds from additional product sales are received. Unmanaged, these imbal-ances can cause temporary shortages of capital. The shortages can cause varying degrees of disruption to the firm and, depending upon other factors (including the severity and timing of the shortage), can permanently damage a firm. With this potential, the importance of effective working capital management becomes obvious.

Understanding the components and movements of working cap-ital and their corresponding effect on cash is important; however, systematic monitoring and forecasting of these activities are equally important. While most firms are required to account for their accounting profits through tax and regulatory compliance report-ing, too often firms do not adequately monitor and forecast cash. Aside from detailed forecasts and budget-to-actual reporting, there are several ratios which can readily be computed from accounting and financial reports that can serve as meaningful indicators and measuring tools for monitoring cash flow.

- Net Working Capital = Current Assets − Current Liabilities.
- Current Ratio = Current Assets/Current Liabilities. This is the most simplistic working capital ratio and is often referred to as a "coverage ratio", as it is often expressed as 1× or 2×, imply-ing that current assets cover current liabilities one or two times. The ratio is used to give an idea of a business' ability to pay back its short-term liabilities (debt and payables) with its short-term assets (cash, inventory, receivables). The higher the current ratio, the more capable the company is of paying its obligations. A ratio under 1 suggests that the company would be unable to pay off its obligations if they came due at that point. The cur-rent ratio, though, cannot be relied upon in isolation as it can be

misleading. It assumes that current assets are liquidated to pay current obligations; however, the current assets in question may have a very different lifespan than the current liabilities. As such, at certain points in time a company may not be able to monetize assets to meet obligations. As a result, examination of the components and duration of the current assets and liabilities is critical when using the current ratio.

- Quick Ratio = (Current Assets − Inventories − Prepaid Expenses)/Current Liabilities. The quick ratio is a more conservative variation of the current ratio. It is also a more well-known liquidity measure because it excludes inventory, which often cannot be converted to cash quickly without a sizable discount, from current assets. In the event that short-term obligations need to be paid off immediately, there are situations in which the current ratio would overestimate a company's short-term financial strength, as discussed previously.
- Inventory Turnover = Cost of Goods Sold in the Period/Average Inventory in the Period. This ratio shows how many times a company's inventory is turned over in a period. A low turnover implies poor sales and, therefore, excess inventory. A high ratio usually implies strong sales. In some cases, though, a high ratio may be cause for concern, as it may imply that the firm is discounting prices to move inventory. High inventory levels are unhealthy because they represent an investment with a zero rate of return. It also opens the company up to trouble should prices begin to fall.
- Days Sales Outstanding (DSO) = (Accounts Receivable/Total Sales on Credit) × Number of Days in the Period. DSO is a measure of the average number of days that a company takes to collect revenue after a sale has been made. A low DSO number means that it takes a firm fewer days to collect its accounts receivable. A high DSO implies that a company is selling its product to customers on credit, taking longer to collect money and exposing itself to more risk.
- Days Payable Outstanding (DPO) = (Accounts Payable/Cost of Sales) × Number of Days in the Period. DPO is an indicator of how

long a firm is taking to pay its trade creditors. DPO is typically looked at either quarterly or yearly (every 90 or 365 days).

## Considerations When Making Working Capital Management Decisions

### Cash Balances

When planning and forecasting a company's cash conversion cycle, the first decision that needs to be made is the nominal amount of cash that the business will need to keep on hand during the year. This level may vary depending upon the production schedule or seasonality of the business. Businesses must also assess whether they want to utilize short-term lines of credit to supplement cash balances during the year. This may be desirable to a business if it has ready access to capital and if the cost of capital does not impact the business' required return on investment. While a certain level of cash is always required to fund daily operations, businesses often keep an additional amount of cash on hand to take advantage of special situations like discounts on payables and/or unexpected expenses like losses related to thefts, natural disasters, or equipment/plant shutdowns. Depending upon the capital structure of the business, it may elect to keep very little cash on hand and instead draw upon a revolving credit facility to fund operations. Companies with a significant amount of debt that want to minimize their interest expense often employ this type of funding structure. As noted earlier, businesses usually try to avoid holding too much cash as the return on investment from cash balances usually dilutes the overall profitability of the business.

### Credit Terms and Discounts

With an average of 30 to 40 percent[9] of a firm's assets in accounts receivable, A/R is often an area where significant liquidity can be released through management attention and action. Managing and

---

[9] Ann-Maree Moodie, "Managing Cash Flow in Tough Times," *Charter*, 2008, p. 2.

encouraging timely payment from vendors can be an effective way to decrease the amount of funds tied up in working capital, as well as to reduce exposure to credit risk. Offering discounts is a common method employed to accelerate payments. However, discounting directly impacts a company's margins and cash receipts. For example, if a business offers a standard 2-percent discount for payment within 10 days on a $1 million payable, it will equate to a $20,000 decrease in the business' bottom line. If necessary, a business may reduce standard terms to improve cash flow, although this can be a double-edged sword as it may adversely affect the business' competitiveness and impact vendor relationships. Until recently, liquidity and credit were readily available, and payment terms gradually grew from 30 to 45 to 60 or even 90 days in certain cases. As businesses were stretched, invoice discounting and factoring became an important tool to improve cash flow and release working capital. Many businesses also look to sell their receivables at a discount to a third party, eliminating the burdensome process of monitoring and collecting on the accounts while simultaneously accelerating cash flow. However, this discount must be carefully weighed against the economic benefit of collecting the cash early.

*Inventory Levels*

A firm's success and profitability depend upon its ability to sell its products or services. For manufacturing firms, inventories must be available to meet production demands. Since sales depend on numerous internal and external factors, inventory management can be as much an art as it is a science. When determining optimal levels of inventory stocks, sales and production forecasts must be continually reviewed and updated. If a business keeps inventory levels too low, it will result in increased costs in the form of overtime and expedited freight charges to meet delivery deadlines; worse yet, it could lead to lost sales and delays for customers. On the other hand, since holding inventory involves costs such as storage and insurance expenses, excess inventory must be avoided if the goal is to maximize profits. If a business is in a position of net debt (i.e., debt exceeds cash), then the excess inventories will also carry a cost of capital expense.

## Common Pitfalls of Companies

*Failure to Properly Assess the Creditworthiness of Customers and Suppliers*

While most transactions with customers and suppliers are governed by contracts, the ability and intention of third parties to honor these contracts can and often do change. It is the obligation of the counterparty to monitor these changes to determine if the supplier or customer poses excessive risk to the business. Depending upon the size of the firm and the number of suppliers or customers, these relationships should be monitored as frequently as possible. Businesses should review financial statements, payment history, business collateral, and business plans when establishing credit terms and collection policies. If a third party becomes excessively risky to a business but is a critical counterparty, the business may elect to factor that specific vendor to protect its financial interest. Working capital forecasts should always expect a certain level of default on receivables.

*Supplier and Customer Concentration*

If a business invests too much of its working capital into any one supplier or customer, it may become difficult to meet funding demands if the third party changes terms or is unable to satisfy payment obligations. Depending upon the nature of a firm's product, it may not be able to adequately diversify its supplier and customer base. In this case, it is important for the business to increase its diligence on the third party. If necessary, the company should also obtain insurance from customers in the form of letters of credit. For concentrated suppliers, businesses have little immediate recourse to suppliers that are unable to deliver products or services, but can protect their cash availability by putting in place short-term funding facilities or maintaining a risk-weighted level of cash-equivalent investments specifically for supplier disruptions.

*Discounting Receivables to Accelerate Cash Conversion*

As previously discussed, discounting receivables is a double-edged sword. While it does accelerate vendor payments, it also impacts margins and gross receipts. Companies must carefully weigh the long-term economic implications of discounting, especially when it becomes standard practice. It is easy for businesses to be slowly lured into discounting without noticing the impact of the incremental economics. Firms may also find it hard to take away discounts from vendors once they are offered.

### Lack of Asset and Liability Matching

As working capital is comprised of both assets and liabilities, managing the balance between them is critical. In a steady-state environment (i.e., stable market conditions and normal business growth), balancing a business' assets and liabilities is not that difficult as market forces often do much of the work. However, in times of high market volatility or business growth, balancing assets and liabilities can be extremely difficult. Firms must continually monitor their capital structure to allow flexibility for external shocks to the system, like the one currently being experienced. In times of high growth, businesses must carefully forecast and monitor the growth of assets and liabilities to avoid shortages of capital, which can cause disruption to a business' operation and profitability.

### Failure to Forecast and Adjust for Seasonality

Many businesses operate in highly seasonal environments and, as such, require varying degrees of working capital throughout the year. Failure to adequately identify and plan for these swings can disrupt a business' operations. Equally important, if a business carries too much working capital in slow periods, it will drive down the business' efficiency and profitability.

### Overengineering Cash Management Systems

As is the case with all things, too much of a good thing can be detrimental. The same holds true for working capital management. Many businesses, in their quest to maximize efficiency and profitability, overengineer their systems. This often leads to unnecessary confusion and work for managers. Firms need to implement working capital strategies that are easy to implement and track, and that are flexible enough to adapt to an ever-changing economy.

## Summary

If "cash is king", then working capital is the "queen" and, just like in the game of chess, she is more complicated in her movements and more powerful in what she can do. Working capital is the lifeblood of all businesses, and is affected directly and indirectly by almost every aspect of the business. A company cannot function without working capital and, if mismanaged, it can potentially lead to the firm's demise. In times of economic prosperity, sound working capital management will allow a business to maximize profits or expand to meet the demands of its customers. In turbulent times, it will allow a business to weather the storm and capitalize on competitors' missteps.

## Selected Additional References

Ann-Maree Moodie, "Managing Cash Flow in Tough Times," *Charter*, 2008, pp. 1–3.

Karen Hawkins and Kathleen Dolan, *Intermediate Accounting*, 8th ed., John Wiley & Sons, Inc., Hoboken, NJ, 1995, pp. 1305–1307.

## B. Barry L. Kasoff and Kenneth B. Furry — A Cash-based Approach to Better Business Information

One of the great truisms in business is that decisions depend on accurate financial information. An executive must have good-quality information about his or her company in order to choose the right course. Without accurate data, no task is done well — whether it be strategic leadership or any of the myriad day-to-day decisions like staffing, pricing, sales of business units, crisis resolutions, etc. Most businesses strive to maintain absolute integrity in their systems and financial information.

We have found, however, that the data that executives and their subordinates use are sometimes lacking in accuracy. Figures that should be consistent across an entire organization may vary depending on which division or business unit produces them. Amounts that should reconcile neatly among different accounts do not. Executives may find themselves struggling to understand and resolve multiple discrepancies without having any systematic way of correcting the problem. If the issue of inaccurate data persists or becomes chronic, it can drive both performance and morale downward. The challenge can become particularly acute in a crisis-management scenario, when lenders are unhappy with management's financial data and the future of the enterprise is at stake.

In the course of fulfilling multiple executive and consulting roles, we have had to face the problem of inaccurate business data many times. The companies in which this scenario has occurred have invariably used accrual-basis accounting and financial systems. Early in his career, one of the authors realized he needed a reliable, systematic tool to use to check for and restore accuracy. The tool had to be effective under time pressure, and the results needed to be credible. What better brick to use to build a more solid foundation, he thought, than *cash*?

## The Nature of Cash

Cash is not subjective; you either have it or you don't. It is usually not hard to tell when you receive or spend it. You know where it is kept, and it is relatively easy to reconcile information about it — everything must tie back to bank or other account statements.

Unlike accrual-basis information, cash is an objective measure of activity. It is rarely a source of confusion, or the subject of judgments, estimates, or deep policy debates about how to report it. It can be used as the information backbone for an organization, from which accrual-basis information can be generated or against which it can be validated.

How can executives use cash information to go about building a better information reality? If time pressure is severe, and accuracy and credibility are at stake, what methodology can be used? One of the authors created a model consisting of eight business equations, to which he applied his company's cash data in a systematic reconciliation process. Each equation was a basic "accounting truth". The cash figures the author's company was using either matched the results of the reconciliation, or they didn't. Each figure that did not match was a "red flag" indicating a need for analysis. By performing the reconciliation process month by month, and working through the "red flag" analyses as they appeared, the author was able to establish a base of accurate information for his company that earned the trust of fellow executives and of owners, directors, employees, lenders, and other stakeholders.

We have applied this cash-based reconciliation process successfully across a wide range of businesses. Some of the companies have faced critical problems of inaccurate information. Others have not, but even at those companies the process has proved to be a confidence builder. The process can be used in any company, whether large or small, public or private. It is particularly useful when accrual-basis information is mistrusted and an executive is under pressure. The process may not be helpful in a business that does not have significant accuracy problems in its financial data and systems.

### The Value of Cash-based Reconciliation

The reconciliation model described in this article has proved to be invaluable in ensuring a foundation of accurate, readily available information for making business decisions at companies in a range of industries. This model was born out of necessity to meet the need for a tool that would systematically confront the problem of inaccurate financial data. The model has been used successfully at public and private companies to test existing data in easy-to-understand business formulas. The testing process forces discrepancies to the surface. Once the discrepancies are resolved, doubt and controversy surrounding financial information dissipate and executives have a solid basis on which to make decisions. Cash-based reconciliation enables any executive to create a better "information truth" for his or her company. To illustrate the model in action, this article focuses on the most compelling of business scenarios: the turnaround.

## *Turnarounds: A Bad Situation Made Worse*

Invariably, turnarounds involve insufficient cash flow with urgency to reduce cash shortfalls very quickly. The "almost out of cash" mindset creates stress that can threaten the clarity of analysis needed to save a business. Lenders also change their focus, shifting away from a normal review of accrual-basis reports to the pressing need to get an accurate picture of cash flow. The cash challenge is often compounded by financial information that has become a matter of contention. Information can vary for a number of reasons, including who is generating it. Figures that should be consistent and tie out with other amounts sometimes do not. Unless inconsistencies are resolved, "information malaise" can set in. Chronic disagreements as to which amounts are correct make matters worse.

### *Crisis Scenario*

As a freshly hired CEO, you arrive on the scene in early June 2009 knowing that your new company has been suffering cash deficiencies for several years. The audited financial statements for 2008 include a "going concern" qualification, and the company is in a crisis, fighting for survival. You rapidly review operations and form a preliminary opinion about the overall strategic direction. Within two weeks, you propose an initial, broadly conceptual turnaround plan that includes recommendations to resolve several obvious problems quickly. By mid-July, the company will have to reduce its labor force by as much as one third. Further drastic corrections must be formulated and implemented by the end of July — just seven weeks after your arrival date. You must propose detailed turnaround measures you believe in, and win the consent of the major lenders as part of a forbearance agreement. If the measures are successfully implemented by the end of November, the company will gain a valuable opportunity to comply with loan covenants, adjust its strategic direction, and create a plan to reconfigure its core business.

*Broken Communications*

The lenders were patient as the company worked to reverse its downward spiral, but because of the regular cash shortfalls the relationship has soured. To make matters worse, the lending officers inform you that they consider the company's financial data to be suspect and that they no longer have confidence in management's financial information. Meaningful communication is beginning to break down. The lenders want definitive information about the company's cash position and solid estimates of cash to be received, but the company's information does not satisfy them. Based on your own survey of the company's financial controls and information systems, you conclude that the lenders' frustrations are mainly valid. You have also heard complaints from the company's managers about the poor quality of some of the information they are forced to work with.

You are expected to present your own analysis at meetings scheduled for the third week of June and in mid-July, and you need to speak with confidence. Your presentations will be a critical step in the company's attempts to gain the lenders' willing cooperation. Your analysis will also be the basis for your formulation of a definitive turnaround plan to propose during the latter part of July. You are aware that everyone needs to feel a solution is coming — soon.

*Cash Data and a Powerful Model*

You can dramatically improve this scenario by using a cash-based reconciliation process. By applying the company's data to the model in Table 16.1, you can create a bridge between relatively trusted historical data, which can serve as an opening balance, and a current closing balance that will reveal the real financial position of the company. Once the bridge is established, management and the lenders will have the same accurate data in hand, and will be able to communicate and cooperate on solid ground.

The model in Table 16.1 has eight components. Six involve the balance sheet and one involves the payroll account. The eighth

Table 16.1 Cash-based Testing and Reconciliation Model — January 2009.

| | | | Cross-Refs. | Schedule Amounts | Model Sums | Variance |
|---|---|---|---|---|---|---|
| I. | | Cash | | | | |
| 1 | | Opening balance of cash account | | $2,500,000 | $2,500,000 | $0 |
| 2 | **plus** | **Cash collections from accounts receivable** | 1 | | **20,500,000** | |
| 3 | plus | Cash collections from other than accounts receivable | | | 500,000 | |
| 4 | plus | Borrowing from bank(s) | 5 | | 18,000,000 | |
| 5 | less | Cash disbursements to vendors of inventory | 3 | | 4,500,000 | |
| 6 | less | Cash disbursements to vendors of other than inventory | 4 | | 3,500,000 | |
| 7 | less | Transfer of funds to payroll account | 7 | | 9,010,000 | |
| 8 | less | Payments to bank(s) | 6 | | 21,000,000 | |
| 9 | less | Other payments | | | 1,000,000 | |
| 10 | | **Ending balance of cash account** | **RED FLAG NO. 1** | **$2,490,000** | **$2,020,000** | **$470,000** |
| II. | | Accounts Receivable | | | | |
| 11 | | Opening balance of accounts receivable | | $50,000,000 | $50,000,000 | $0 |
| 12 | plus | Gross sales | 11 | | 20,000,000 | |
| 13 | **less** | **Cash collections from accounts receivable** | 1 | | **20,500,000** | |
| 14 | less | Credits to accounts receivable | 12 | | 500,000 | |

(*Continued*)

Table 16.1　(*Continued*)

| | | Cross-Refs. | Schedule Amounts | Model Sums | Variance |
|---|---|---|---|---|---|
| **15** | **Ending balance of accnts. receivable** | **RED FLAG NO. 2** | **$49,000,000** | **$49,470,000** | **$(470,000)** |
| III. | Finished Goods Inventory | | | | |
| 16 | Opening balance of finished goods inventory | | $90,000,000 | $90,000,000 | $0 |
| 17 plus | Purchases of finished goods inventory | 2 | | 4,000,000 | |
| 18 plus | Usage of raw material inventory | 10 | | 4,000,000 | |
| 19 plus | Payment of payroll for production of inventory | 8 | | 2,000,000 | |
| 20 plus | Charges of overhead to finished goods inventory | | | 2,000,000 | |
| 21 less | Cost of goods sold | 13 | | 10,000,000 | |
| 22 | Ending balance of finished goods inventory | **RECONCILED** | **$92,000,000** | **$92,000,000** | **$0** |
| IV. | Raw Material Inventory | | | | |
| 23 | Opening balance of raw material inventory | | $12,000,000 | $12,000,000 | $0 |
| 24 plus | Purchases of raw material inventory | 9 | | 3,000,000 | |
| 25 less | Usage of raw material inventory | 10 | | 4,000,000 | |
| 26 | Ending balance of raw material inventory | **RECONCILED** | **$11,000,000** | **$11,000,000** | **$0** |
| V. | Accounts Payable | | | | |

(*Continued*)

Table 16.1 (*Continued*)

| | | | Cross-Refs. | Schedule Amounts | Model Sums | Variance |
|---|---|---|---|---|---|---|
| 27 | | Opening balance of accounts payable | | $25,000,000 | $25,000,000 | $0 |
| 28 | plus | Purchases of finished goods inventory | 2 | | 4,000,000 | |
| 29 | plus | Purchases of raw material inventory | 9 | | 3,000,000 | |
| 30 | plus | Purchases of other than inventory | | | 500,000 | |
| 31 | less | Cash disbursements to vendors of inventory | 3 | | 4,500,000 | |
| 32 | less | Cash disbursements to vendors of other than inventory | 4 | | 3,500,000 | |
| 33 | less | Credits to accounts payable | | | 100,000 | |
| 34 | | Ending balance of accounts payable | **RECONCILED** | **$24,400,000** | **$24,400,000** | $0 |
| VI. | | Bank Loan(s) | | | | |
| 35 | | Opening balance of bank loan(s) | | $200,000,000 | $200,000,000 | $0 |
| 36 | plus | Borrowing from bank(s) | 5 | | 18,000,000 | |
| 37 | plus | Interest | | | 1,250,000 | |
| 38 | plus | Bank fees | | | 50,000 | |
| 39 | less | Payments to bank(s) | | | 21,000,000 | |
| 40 | | Ending balance of bank loan(s) | **RECONCILED** | **$198,300,000** | **$198,300,000** | $0 |
| VII. | | Payroll | | | | |
| 41 | | Opening balance of payroll account | | $50,000 | $50,000 | $0 |

(*Continued*)

Table 16.1   (*Continued*)

|  |  |  | Cross-Refs. | Schedule Amounts | Model Sums | Variance |
|---|---|---|---|---|---|---|
| 42 | plus | Transfer of funds to payroll account | 7 | | 9,010,000 | |
| 43 | less | Payment of payroll for production of inventory | 8 | | 2,000,000 | |
| 44 | less | Payment of payroll for other than production of inventory | | | 7,000,000 | |
| 45 | less | Payroll services administrative fees | | | 10,000 | |
| 46 | | Ending balance of payroll account | **RECONCILED** | **$50,000** | **$50,000** | $0 |
| VIII. | | Gross Profit | | | | |
| 47 | | Gross sales | **11** | | $20,000,000 | |
| 48 | less | Credits to accounts receivable | **12** | | 500,000 | |
| 49 | | Net sales | | | $19,500,000 | |
| 50 | less | Cost of goods sold | 13 | | 10,000,000 | |
| 51 | | Gross profit | | | $ 9,500,000 | |
| 52 | | Gross margin | | 48.7% | 48.7% | |

component, Gross Profit, is included as a control check on the entire reconciliation. The Cash component, item I in the table, is central because all cash receipts and disbursements flow through that account.

Each of the components is a standard business formula — a basic "business truth". The model uses 39 data points, 13 of which occur twice and are the "common" data points. Because of the common data points, the model is self-checking: the direct and indirect interdependency of the components through the common data points makes it virtually impossible for the reconciliation process not to catch any error. A problem in one component, if not detected right away, will come to light in the reconciliation of one or more other components.

The model does not use any accrual-basis accounting concepts, thereby deliberately eliminating the subjectivity that is part of accrual-basis accounting. The model tests objective factual information — how much cash was on hand, how much was received and spent, and how much remains.

*A Systematic Solution — Getting the Data*

You begin the reconciliation process using the company's year-end 2008 audited balance sheet as the starting point, because this information has been largely accepted. You will roll the reconciliation forward **month by month** through June 2009. Your team sets up the model on a spreadsheet. Gathering data for a common data point will populate the model wherever that data point appears in the eight components.

*Building the Reconciliation*

Once the model is populated for January 2009, the spreadsheet adds all of the detailed data from the company's schedules and presents the resulting sums for the 52 line items under the "Model Sums" column (see Table 16.1). Next to that column, the "Schedule Amounts" column shows the actual totals recorded in the company's schedules. By comparing the "Model Sums" and "Schedule Amounts" columns, you know immediately whether the amounts in the company's schedules agree with the model. Each model sum that does not match the corresponding schedule amount is a red flag, indicating that further work is required to achieve reconciliation. Each red flag is analyzed to understand the discrepancy and correct or explain it.

*Model-based Analysis*

The reconciliation process itself can be used as a roadmap for analysis. The following example is simplified in order to illustrate a single problem-solving journey, but it is realistic because it is a composite of actual experiences of the authors.

The model is now fully populated with data for January 2009. All of the components reconcile except for Cash and Accounts Receivable. This means that the model's sums for the five reconciling components — Finished Goods Inventory, Raw Material Inventory, Accounts Payable, Bank Loan(s), and Payroll — exactly match the corresponding totals from the company's schedules. It also means that the model's Gross Profit component reconciles with the gross profit figure in the company's financial statements. In reality, six components would rarely, if ever, reconcile in the first attempt.

*Red Flags*

The first red flag is that the ending balance of Cash from the company's schedules is $2,490,000, but the model's sum for Cash is only $2,020,000 (line 10 in Table 16.1). The variance is a positive $470,000. The second red flag is that the ending balance of Accounts Receivable from the schedules is $49,000,000, while the model's sum is $49,470,000 (line 15). That variance is a negative $470,000. So, Cash is low and Accounts Receivable are high by the same amount.

You note that two of the five data points included in Accounts Receivable, "gross sales" and "credits to accounts receivable", also appear in Gross Profit (see cross-references 11 and 12 under components II and VIII). The Gross Profit component has no red flags, so you consider the "gross sales" and "credits to accounts receivable" amounts to be presumptively valid. You focus on the only data point that appears in both the Accounts Receivable and Cash components: "cash collections from accounts receivable" of $20,500,000 (lines 2 and 13). Nothing is outwardly suspicious about this amount, but your analysis and instinct tell you the problem may lurk there. Your internal team discovers that cash deposits for one customer, Acme Corporation, were recorded in the company's schedules at $1,040,000 instead of the actual amount of $570,000, an overstatement of $470,000. Your team makes the correction by using the $570,000 amount. The Cash and Accounts Receivable components now reconcile, and the two red flags are gone.

## *Big Ramifications*

Your opportunities to explore the ramifications flowing from this process are just beginning. The first inference you draw is that the company's records and accounting processes are not as good as they should be. You also make assessments of the strengths and weaknesses of a number of the company's managers. In the process of resolving the red flags, you have had a chance to see these managers in action. You have seen how the managers perform — how they approach problems, and how they interact with each other and their subordinates. You have formed an opinion as to the suitability of these managers for guiding the company's turnaround efforts, which will be useful in your staffing decisions.

## *Hard Conclusions*

You continue to analyze and realize that the company's profitability from Acme, its customer, in January 2009 was much lower than the company had thought. You review sales to Acme in that month and discover that at $570,000, they were equal to that month's cash collections from Acme. You know that the cost of goods sold to Acme in January was $513,000. So, the cash-basis gross margin for Acme in January was not $527,000 ($1,040,000 less $513,000), as formerly believed, but only $57,000 ($570,000 less $513,000). That is a huge swing: the cash-basis gross margin has plummeted from over 50 percent to just 10 percent. You must accept that Acme was actually a low-margin customer during January 2009.

*Impact on Profitability*

This reality carries implications for profitability. Your team's work shows that, for the year to date, the margin for Acme was lower than the company had believed. The team discovers that the company has been giving Acme and nine other customers unusually low pricing. Upon investigation, the cause of the problem turns out to be incorrect coding for this entire category of customers. Acme and the other nine customers were supposed to be receiving a standard discount of 5 percent. Because of the coding error, however, they were receiving an inappropriately large discount of 50 percent. Contrary to what the company had believed, its dealings with all 10 customers have been unprofitable for several years. The company realizes it has been relying on bad data, and corrects the coding. Now, it must approach each of the 10 customers and bring the pricing offered to them in line with its actual pricing. Some of the customers may continue to purchase from the company, but at the actual, higher prices; others — all low-margin customers — will drop out. In either case, the company's overall profitability will improve.

*Layers of Analysis*

Like concentric circles expanding from a few stones thrown into a pond, the model enables you to build layer upon layer of analysis. Each time the model identifies a problem, you extrapolate from it into related or other areas to check for similar problems. The model empowers you to draw logical inferences, troubleshoot, and explore solutions widely beyond the immediate context.

*Foundation for a Turnaround — Good Data Means Better Communication*

You and your team move on to February, March, etc., until the process is finished through June 2009. When the entire reconciliation task has been completed, you have built a "validation bridge" from the audited December 31, 2008 information to data as of June 30, 2009. The level of accuracy you have achieved empowers you to formulate and propose a detailed turnaround plan. This achievement is not lost on the lenders. During your presentation to them in mid-July, your confidence in the information underlying your financial analysis is evident to all. Communication with the lenders improves dramatically. The reconciliation process has enabled the company to speak the language the lenders use in times of financial crisis: cash. You and the company make significant progress on the detailed turnaround plan, and present it to the lenders in late July. Based on the detailed plan and your responses to their questions, the lenders indicate that they will agree to another forbearance arrangement.

*Creating a Cashbook and Accrual-Basis Statements*

While the definitive turnaround plan is under implementation, your team continues to use the model to test the company's data each month. They place the cash-basis output from the model in a cashbook on your desk. You instruct your team to use the schedules in the cashbook to create the company's internal accrual-basis financial statements each month. They add, at the bottom of each schedule in the cashbook, appropriate entries tying the cash-basis results to the internal accrual-basis statements. Your confidence soars.

## Putting First Things First

Why use a reconciliation process to determine what to work on? Why not perform an overall assessment of a business, interview managers in relevant business units, prioritize the areas to focus on, and begin to investigate and analyze? In our example, why not move directly to reviewing the company's pricing? The answer lies in the fact that a decision maker must know that the information he or she is using is valid. Relying on dubious information to perform important work is not the wisest path. The model puts the testing of information first. Achieving a level of accuracy and confidence in information should still be the top priority, even when the pressure to act is severe. Recognizing this, the manager or consultant who decides to test information can at the same time *use the testing process itself* to force problems into the open.

### The Hard Way Is Often the Right Way

The process described here is not the norm. Executives can generally recognize when information softness is a problem, and diagnose whether an accuracy issue is systemic or more limited. But sometimes they do not attack the problem of inaccurate data head-on, and just decide to "deal with it" in a not-too-rigorous way. They do not confront the problem systematically, and to some extent may knowingly tolerate questionable information. They may believe that correction is impossible except through a full-scale external audit.

However, accuracy in data is not optional. If executives tolerate soft data, they should recognize that the course they are setting for their company could lead in the wrong direction, or progress at a slower pace, because of the distorted information. That is a real risk. Testing data with this model can go a long way toward solving that risk. Even under the most urgent time pressure, model-based testing using cash data makes accuracy possible. Using the model is more difficult than not using it; achieving greater accuracy requires more effort. But better accuracy means a better foundation, and truth is the only solid place on which to stand.

## C. Baker Smith, CTP — The Balance Sheet Made Me Do It: Killing the Company by Squeezing Cash

"I am a balance sheet guy," a company owner said to me after I tried to explain the importance of positive cash flow to his technology company. He made it clear that he managed the balance sheet, not cash, and would continue to do so even though his company was bleeding cash and about to hit the wall. As a graduate of one of the top universities in the U.S., he was extremely bright and had an excellent grasp of the company and its industry segment. In fact, his response is typical since many owners and investors share his viewpoint.

Over the years, he had enjoyed considerable success with several companies by utilizing balance sheet metrics. As he nurtured and grew companies with careful attention to the balance sheet, he was able to sell such companies at very attractive returns on investment.

So why trifle with success? Indeed, the Harvard Business Press publication, "The Magic of Balancing the Balance Sheet"[10] ("Harvard article"), describes the process. This article is an excellent primer with good, practical advice for the company manager who is willing to actually read, digest, and implement the steps outlined. However, the notion that managing the balance sheet alone is a shortcut to success is too beguiling for many otherwise hardworking decision makers. Some "balance sheet guys" actually believe that managing the balance sheet will magically solve all of the company's issues. One of the most extreme views of management by balance sheet is that financial performance may be improved without having to resort to increasing sales or cutting costs. Really?

To a manager, one of the attractions of the strictly balance sheet approach to management is that it is somewhat detached from the nitty-gritty of running a business. However, financial managers who take the time to digest the Harvard article realize that its emphasis is on working capital. It defines working capital as current assets minus current liabilities. Current assets are defined as cash, accounts receivable, and inventory; while current liabilities include accounts payable and short-term loan payments.[11] In fact, these components are precisely the elements on which turnaround consultants focus in a cash crisis. Moreover, when a cash-burning company carries an asset-based working capital loan, the current assets of cash, receivables, and inventory, along with any operating losses, interact in a dynamic way to determine the company's cash availability on a daily basis. When factored into a forward-looking cash flow projection on a 13-week or other period, the working capital and availability calculations

---

[10]Karen Berman, Joe Knight, and John Case, "The Magic of Balancing the Balance Sheet," excerpted from *Financial Intelligence: A Manager's Guide to What the Numbers Really Mean*, Harvard Business Press, Cambridge, MA, 2005.
[11]*Ibid.*

can forecast cash shortfalls and predict when the company will hit the wall.

In the case of the technology company, one of the ways the owner sought to control working capital was to direct managers to not write checks to certain vendors. Given that the company was struggling with operating losses and tight cash, there was some logic to his approach since a cash-strapped company will be unable to write checks at some point in time when there is no money left in the bank to cover them. However, balance-sheet-only managers typically do not appreciate precisely where they are within the restructuring cycle, mistakenly assuming that multiple-step events have already occurred simply because the manager can foresee them on the balance sheet. The step that got left out in the case of the technology company was prioritizing cash for "keep the doors open" expenses. In short order, the company's landlord sued them and other essential vendors threatened to cut off critical services and repossess equipment. Thus, ill-conceived actions to manage working capital actually accelerated cash demands and confronted management with a full-blown crisis.

The genesis of the "freeze the checks" approach to cash management is a corruption of the "manage to cash" approach used by turnaround consultants. Since a company cannot spend cash it does not have, and should not intentionally write bad checks, turnaround consultants typically use a "manage to cash" approach to prioritize expenditures. Top-of-the-list status typically goes to payroll and payroll taxes, as well as fiduciary withholdings such as health insurance, 401(k) plans, child support, and garnishments; this is followed by payroll-like expenses such as sales force commissions, employee expenses, and fees paid to employee-like contractors and consultants. Meanwhile, the financial advisor looks for ways to increase sales and profits and to cut costs, while seeking outside capital by redeploying assets and by requesting additional funds from owners and lenders.

The mutation from the "manage to cash" approach to the "freeze the checks" approach omits several crucial steps, inclusive of prioritizing payables as well as increasing profitable sales and cutting costs. For example, a furniture company utilized the "freeze the checks" approach after a turnaround team had brought the company to break even. As a cost-saving measure, the company handed the reins over to interim managers who referred to themselves as turnaround managers, but were essentially out-of-work executives. Opining that the company had left too much money on the table, the interim managers put a several-month hold on all payables except payroll, only easing open the cash spigot when creditors screamed. The furniture company was so weakened by this trauma that the business was sold within a year with little financial return to ownership. While interim management argued that they were just controlling the balance sheet by squeezing working capital, the turnaround slipped away from them.

Even the Harvard article does not support this method of blind management of working capital. It calls for analysis and management of individual components of working capital, meaning that managing only cash would not be enough. For example, the Harvard article requires the manager to look at accounts receivable as one of the individual components of current assets in working capital. Moreover, it requires the manager to look beyond the gross amount of receivables to a measure of collectability of receivables, days sales outstanding (DSO), which tracks the average age of receivables in days. Furthermore, the Harvard article requires analysis beyond DSO to see which particular receivables are aging out and may need quick intervention with customers in order to collect.[12] A company's aged-out receivables are also problematic in asset-based loans because they may become ineligible for borrowing and thereby reduce the cash availability under the loan facility. Therefore, the authentic balance sheet manager will be intimately involved with all aspects of working capital, including cash, receivables, inventory, and payables.

A true balance sheet manager would never simply freeze cash. The Harvard article describes balance sheet management as a *balancing* of working capital, i.e., current assets minus current liabilities. Put another way, current assets like cash, receivables, and inventory are added; while current liabilities like payables are subtracted.

---

[12] *Ibid.*

What happens to payables if cash is frozen? As long as the company continues to operate and bring in raw materials and labor while no cash goes out the door to pay suppliers, accounts payable will typically increase. Based on the law of addition and subtraction, holding cash and other current assets steady while deducting an increased payables amount would result in a net decrease in working capital. How will a manager know that working capital has net decreased in a cash-tight situation? Like the technology company, he or she will experience an explosion of creditor problems.

What could be done to counteract the flawed approach of the balance sheet guy and prevent the technology company from cratering? Although some managers believe balance sheet management is so magical that the company will never have to be concerned with increasing sales or cutting costs, that is precisely what is required. For example, a consumer product company was giving the turnaround team pushback against recommended operating improvements. Rather than implement specific steps that would improve operations and cut the cost of goods sold, they argued that they could make any improvement ownership needed by forcing down inventory, but laughingly said that they would bring inventory back up again after the month's end. These balance sheet guys completely missed the point. Contraction and expansion of inventory would have been a superficial and temporary change to a single element of working capital, while the operating changes under consideration would have brought real cash into the company by increasing profit and would thereby have increased the company's value.

In the case of the technology company, management bit the bullet and, after a bottom-up review of profitability, eliminated losing business lines and their associated employee and overhead costs. The company further undertook a buildup of its profitable business lines. The profitability of the new business was validated because it was based upon additional sales not taken from competitors and was not the result of price discounting. The combination of cost cuts and increased sales at a profit was sufficient to restore the technology company to profitability in just a few months.

Nevertheless, cash management is not just an end in itself. The purpose of prioritizing and controlling cash is to buy time necessary to find a solution which will maximize realization on the company's assets and business. Hopefully, this solution will produce a turnaround, or perhaps a combination of a buildup of performing business lines and a redeployment of underperforming business lines and associated assets and costs. Balance sheet management that skips the prioritization of cash frequently backfires. If essential trade creditors are all treated as potential candidates for a haircut, they will respond with whatever leverage they have. If they have a service or product without which the company cannot survive, they may begin to curtail the service or product unless the company makes arrangements to pay them, thus depriving the company of time needed to turn around.

Negotiation is a typical strength of a balance sheet guy. He negotiates when he buys companies, and he negotiates when he sells companies. Depending on his style, he may negotiate right up to the closing table. Consequently, he may come to regard negotiation as having brought millions of additional dollars to the bottom line.

Because of his success at negotiation, the technology company's owner directed company management to negotiate with virtually every stakeholder, including trade creditors. Unfortunately, creditors are reluctant to negotiate with a debtor that is already behind on its bills. While these negotiations can sometimes be successful, creditors are typically expecting some upside, perhaps some catch-up payments, interest, or success fee. If a discount is requested without upfront cash, the creditors may regard the negotiation as a waste of time or, worse, not in good faith. Once company-initiated negotiations appear to be not in good faith, their lack of credibility tends to render further negotiation futile. Remember the technology company — its lack of credibility led to a breakdown in negotiations with its landlord, and the company was faced with a potential lockout of its business premises. In a short time, the company's "freeze the checks" approach transformed the situation from tight cash to severe crisis.

Negotiation by a balance sheet guy can take on a life of its own. The technology company's management was ordered to negotiate with everyone: employees as well as employee-like contractors. While employee pay cuts may be on the table in the right circumstances, this should be in the context of an overall turnaround plan. Individuals who provide services to a company over a period of time do not typically expect to renegotiate their payment with management after services have been rendered. Such management behavior may even be unethical. As Scripture indicates, an employee deserves his paycheck and this payment should not be held up, not even for one night.[13]

Contracting out is a growing practice when a company may need to service seasonal or peak customers on a weekly, daily, or hourly basis without having to manage payroll expansion and contraction, along with the attendant taxes, fringe benefits, training expenses, and overhead costs. Nevertheless, the company's contractors need to be treated like employees, not creditors, for pay purposes because they have their own obligations to meet. Just as the company expects their services, the contractors expect to work and get paid. If the contractors do not get paid, the company should not expect them to continue working. Balance sheet guys who believe this scenario is appropriate for negotiation do not know when to stop.

Balance sheet guys also tend to negotiate with their professionals, including lawyers and financial advisors. The company typically reasons that a professional so values the relationship that negotiation of a reduced compensation agreement is normal and acceptable. This view overlooks the fact that a professional sells his or her services on the basis of time. Although a professional could have sold the same period of time to someone else, the hours have already been devoted to the company that later decided to negotiate. As a practical matter, such negotiation tends to destroy the client–professional relationship because a client typically becomes uncomfortable seeking the advice and counsel of the professional once the client has categorized the professional as just another creditor. As the bond is gradually broken,

---

[13]1 Timothy 5:16: "The laborer is worthy of his wages"; Leviticus 19:13: "Do not hold back the wages of a hired man overnight."

the company becomes weakened since it no longer has the assistance of its former, experienced advisor. While a company should monitor and control professional costs, it is typically hurting itself when it decides to negotiate a haircut with its professionals.

Turning a company around often requires restructuring of trade debt. For example, a cable converter company needed to restructure its accounts payable. While smaller payables were quickly paid to eliminate nuisance and to save time, larger creditors were given the option of full payment in installments or a one-time discounted cash payment. There can be many variations to this approach to restructuring payables, but two things are necessary for success: a turnaround and cash. The restructuring cannot be accomplished unless the company returns to profitability and has some excess liquidity, either generated internally from profits or contributed from external sources such as investors or lenders. A restructuring plan cannot be accomplished if the company continues to run losses. For their part, creditors must agree to provide goods or services on mutually workable credit terms.

Some companies get the idea that bankruptcy can be used to force trade creditors to take a reduced debt settlement. However, if the company attempts to accomplish a payables restructuring in bankruptcy without some cash or a believable payment plan for trade creditors, the company will likely be sold or liquidated and the ownership equity wiped out.

Cash is the lifeblood of a company and is essential to survival. Even if the company's balance sheet is otherwise robust, the company will die without cash, just as an otherwise virile athlete will die from unchecked bleeding. As the technology company found out, cash — not just the balance sheet — must be carefully managed. Managing cash is a challenge when the company loses more money than it makes. Management must act quickly to stop the bleeding while it increases profitable sales and slashes costs. Payroll and essential services must be funded to keep the company alive until it can be stabilized and returned to profitability. Just as no intelligent, moral person would block emergency vehicles responding to a crash, no authentic manager of a cash-strapped company would stop funding "keep the doors open" expenses based upon some balance sheet rubric. A manager is appointed primarily to control resources and to make decisions. Failure to live up to his or her calling is the lot of the manager who follows rote shortcuts to manage the balance sheet and sidesteps critical thinking and decision making. If such a manager is uncomfortable managing anything other than the balance sheet, he or she should engage a qualified turnaround professional to assist with cash management.

## D. Michael Chartock and Wendy Landon — The Importance of Cash Flow in the Retail Context[14]

The importance of cash flow in the retail context cannot be overstated. In this article, we will suggest five indicators of why cash flow is critical to retailers, and we will offer evidence supporting each of these indicators. Given the extremely constricted credit markets at the time of writing (June 2009), we will pay particular attention to the current retail environment.

### Five Indicators

Each of the following indicators supports our conclusion that cash flow is critical in the retail context:

(1) *Retailers are electing to retain "costly" cash.* Retailers are choosing to retain cash even if the alternative is costly. Retailers are drawing down on available lines of credit even if they do not require the liquidity to fund operations or capital expenditures. In addition, retailers who have the cash to make bond payments and who have the right to pay-in-kind (PIK) through the issuance of additional securities opt to PIK. Or put another way, retailers will choose to pay more (by means of cash interest and fees or in terms of more "expensive" PIK currency) with respect to their lines of credit (cash flow- and asset-based), in order to preserve liquidity.

---

[14]The views expressed by the authors are not necessarily the views of the authors' employer.

(2) *Lack of cash usually leads to quick liquidation.* If a retailer runs out of cash and is not able to access the credit markets, it will have few alternatives to immediate liquidation.

(3) *Cash is the "reason to exist".* Everyday, retailers ask themselves and are asked by their stakeholders, "Does this company have a reason to exist?" In both the healthy company and distressed company contexts, cash flow leading to profitability provides the most compelling affirmative answer for the long term.

(4) *Cash currently is the principal "circuit breaker".* Because lending criteria loosened significantly during the 2005–2008 period (lending covenants were relaxed or even non-existent), the only "circuit breaker" for a retailer today is lack of cash flow leading to the absence of cash to fund operations.

(5) *Cash "war chests" are built heading into bankruptcy.* In the weeks leading up to a bankruptcy filing, retailers will build a "war chest" of cash. Even those retailers for whom liquidation is the likely outcome want cash to avoid administrative insolvency. Thus, in the face of impending bankruptcy, retailers stop paying creditors (secured creditors, unsecured creditors, and landlords), draw down on bank credit lines, and retain whatever cash they can. All the more so for retailers for whom reorganization or a *bona fide* going concern sale is a legitimate option and who want as much flexibility as possible while under the protection of the bankruptcy court.

Each of these factors is strong evidence supporting the importance of cash flow. We will now explore each in more detail.

*Retailers Are Electing to Retain "Costly" Cash*

Retailers are drawing down on available lines of credit even if they do not require the liquidity to fund operations or capital expenditures. Put another way, retailers will choose to pay cash interest and fees with respect to their lines of credit (cash flow- and asset-based) in order to preserve liquidity.

One such example is Ann Taylor Stores Corporation (NYSE: "ANN"). On March 6, 2009, ANN reported its fiscal year 2008 earnings. In a Form 8-K filed with the U.S. Securities and Exchange Commission (SEC), ANN stated:

> Our balance sheet and liquidity position remained strong, and we ended the year with $112 million in cash and no bank debt. In addition, to safeguard against ongoing uncertainty in the credit market, we drew down $125 million of our $250 million revolving credit facility, as a cushion, in the event we need incremental capital in the coming months to cover our typical working capital build for Spring.

When ANN reported its first quarter earnings release on May 20, 2009, the company stated on its earnings call:

> We ended the quarter with $199 million of cash and cash equivalents, of which $125 million reflected the cash drawdown under our $250 million revolver. As you will recall in early March, we made the decision to draw down half of our revolver as a precautionary measure in what was a very uncertain credit market environment. As we indicated at the time, we did not intend to use the cash but to keep it in reserve, and in fact we haven't used it. We will continue to monitor financial market conditions and as the year progresses and we build our cash position, we may choose to pay down all or a portion of the revolver before year end.

This drawdown of the credit line reflected the tumultuous nature of the marketplace at a time when companies were uncertain of the availability of contractual credit lines. More than two months later, ANN was continuing to borrow money and hold cash that it may or may not have needed, rather than risk a potential liquidity squeeze in the future. By maintaining the cash balance and by accessing the credit line, ANN was assuring its vendors that it could pay for merchandise regardless of volatility in the credit markets and despite potentially weak operating results. With this assurance, vendors would continue to ship merchandise (including on more favorable terms than it would give a company with less liquidity), helping ANN reach the critical fourth quarter from which most retailers derive most of their profits. This behavior underscores the importance of a solid cash position and access to liquidity.

Another example of the importance of liquidity can be seen in retailers who have the cash to make bond payments but who have the right to PIK their interest payments and opt to PIK. Or put another way, retailers will pay more to forestall the possibility of near-term future illiquidity. One such company that took advantage of its PIK option was Neiman Marcus, Inc. ("NM"). In its January 9, 2009 Form 8-K filing, NM announced that it would be using its PIK option, stating:

> Given the dislocation in the financial markets and the uncertainty as to when reasonable conditions will return, [NM] believes that conditions remain appropriate to utilize this feature even though [NM] currently has $576.3 million of unused borrowing available under its $600 million revolving credit facility. Accordingly, [NM] has elected to pay PIK interest for the interest period.

On April 9, 2009, NM again issued an 8-K filing stating that it would PIK its next interest payment. Of particular note is the company's cash position on January 31, 2009 and May 2, 2009 of US$223.2 million and US$229.4 million, respectively. Once again, a retailer with seemingly adequate (if not more than adequate) liquidity determined that the value of cash was so great that it would pay more (the PIK payment rate was at 9.75 percent versus a 9.0-percent cash rate for NM) to preserve its cash and credit line availability. Of course, in addition to volatile capital and lending markets, there was heightened concern over profitability and operational performance. By preserving cash, NM (among other retailers) was mitigating the potential of a liquidity squeeze due to weakened sales/results.

It is not a coincidence that retailers are taking these actions in the face of continued weakness in the credit markets and the associated reduced availability of credit. As a point of reference, although the 10-year average leveraged loan spread is about LIBOR + 3.75 percent, over the past 12 months this spread peaked at approximately LIBOR + 15.0 percent and currently remains several hundred basis points above its historical average.

*Lack of Cash Usually Leads to Quick Liquidation*

Of approximately 40 retail Chapter 11 filings since the beginning of 2008 that we reviewed, only two emerged with plans of reorganization (as much smaller players); three are still developing potential plans; and all of the rest were liquidated or sold in a Section 363 sale. High-profile examples of companies that followed the liquidation alternative include Circuit City, Linens 'n Things, Mervyns, and Bombay Company. The reasons for such a high rate of liquidation are several, including: changes in the bankruptcy law significantly tightening deadlines for troubled companies to restructure their businesses and reject leases (thereby making emergence less likely as it is difficult to make decisions in such a short time frame); the fact that aggressive business plans are no longer being supported by lenders; the fact that lenders are charging more for capital and tightening covenants to ensure companies meet their business plans; and, finally, the fact that the U.S. consumer is still struggling in a weak economy which may not be improving any time soon. When taken together, these factors make emerging from bankruptcy much more difficult than in years past.

Investors are hesitant to invest in turnarounds that may or may not occur. If a retailer's business is not throwing off enough cash to pay its obligations to vendors and lenders in a timely manner, the business will likely fail.

Circuit City Stores, Inc. is one example of a company whose decline in profitability and cash flow ultimately led to its liquidation. For the fiscal year ending February 28, 2007, the company generated revenues of US$12.4 billion; generated earnings before interest, taxes, depreciation, and amortization (EBITDA) of US$268.2 million; and had cash of US$739.5 million. For the fiscal year ending February 29, 2008, the company generated US$11.7 billion of revenues, incurred an EBITDA loss of US$157.0 million, and had cash of US$297.4 million. At the end of both February 2007 and 2008, nothing was drawn upon under its credit facility and availability was US$439.9 million and US$967.6 million, respectively. A few years ago, this company may have been a financeable turnaround story.

But, despite a significant revenue base, the company began to burn through its cash. According to the company's SEC reports, by August 31, 2008, cash declined to US$92.5 million with US$215 million drawn upon its credit facility and US$441.9 million of availability. The precipitous decline in cash and EBITDA combined with the credit facility usage caused vendors to restrict trade credit and reduce payment terms, in some cases requiring cash in advance. The key metric in this situation was cash, and the associated credit availability and cash flow (or loss, in this case). Apparently, the company's lenders were concerned about the rate of cash burn and the rapid increase in funding commitments. The company was subsequently unable to obtain additional financing and filed for bankruptcy protection on November 10, 2008. In a relatively short period of time, the company had, according to documents filed in the company's bankruptcy proceedings, drawn down approximately US$900 million under its credit facility. Thus, despite the company's large revenue base, the company's cash and financing positions all but forced bankruptcy and liquidation, with vendors reluctant to ship and alternative financing not readily available.

*Cash Is the "Reason to Exist"*

Cash is like a report card for retailers. Everyone looks at cash flow: boards of directors, senior management, lenders, investment analysts, vendors, factors, appraisers, landlords, bond traders, employees/ unions, investment bankers, politicians, and communities. If cash flow were not a (and in many cases, the) critical factor, it would not be such a critical benchmark for virtually all retail constituents.

The receipt of fresh merchandise keeps customers coming through the doors, and the cycle continues. Everyday, retailers ask themselves and are asked by their stakeholders, "Does this company have a reason to exist?" In both the healthy company and distressed company contexts, cash flow (leading to profitability) provides the most compelling affirmative answer for the long term. "Concept companies" which previously obtained tremendous valuations (online retailers, telecommunications companies, Internet service providers, search engines, satellite media companies, to name a few examples) have seen those valuations collapse, while more traditional ("rational") cash flow retailers such as Wal-Mart and Kohl's have seen their valuations dip more moderately.

*Cash Currently Is the Principal "Circuit Breaker"*

From 2004 to 2008, over US$1.1 trillion of leveraged loans was issued in the institutional marketplace, of which approximately

70 percent (by dollar value) was placed in 2006–2007. During this period of exuberance, a new trend of "covenant-lite" loans emerged. A "covenant-lite" loan is a loan with minimal (or no) maintenance covenants of the type traditionally found in bank loans. These traditional safeguards and "circuit breakers" are used by lenders to ensure that borrowers satisfy their business plans. Monthly and/or quarterly maintenance covenants, among other things, restrict leverage and impose minimum fixed-charge coverage ratios, and typically allow for some reasonable (e.g., 20 percent) variance. Lenders not only put a "canary in the coal mine", but are able to reassess their risk in and exposure to borrowers in times of temporary or intermediate distress. Thus, if a retailer's financial performance deteriorates, it will find itself in default of its covenants and the lenders will have the opportunity to renegotiate the covenants and charge more appropriate pricing to compensate for higher risk. Or, in extreme cases, the lenders may decide not to extend any further credit and may demand payment in full.

During the era of available credit (2006–2007), however, when it became a "borrower's market", retailers were pitting potential lender against potential lender. Retail borrowers were able to obtain not just more favorable interest rates, but more lenient maintenance covenants, 25-percent-plus cushions, or no maintenance covenants at all. In fact, some estimates of the 2006–2007 period suggest that up to US$150 billion of covenant-lite loans was issued. Consequently, although a company may not default as quickly, when a company does default, the deterioration in the business is more likely to be catastrophic and result in liquidation. Recent large retail liquidations including Linens 'n Things and Circuit City are examples of companies whose financial positions were so weak upon filing that the cases resulted in full liquidation.

*Cash "War Chests" Are Built Heading into Bankruptcy*

In the weeks leading up to a bankruptcy filing, retailers typically build a "war chest" of cash. They draw down whatever they can on their bank credit lines, stop paying key creditors (secured creditors, unsecured creditors, and landlords), and stop most capital expenditures. Even those retailers for whom liquidation is the likely outcome will want cash to avoid administrative insolvency. Companies do this in order to maintain some control in discussions with their lenders or potential debtor-in-possession (DIP) lenders. For example, one middle-market consumer products company drew down on its revolver during the third quarter in normal course. At the end of the fourth quarter, however, the company did not repay the revolver, as it had historically done. The current economic meltdown had caused the company to misplan, and the company knew it would be in violation of its credit agreement during the first quarter. Such a breach in covenants would restrict the company's access to its revolver. By keeping the revolver drawn, however, the company had much-needed liquidity which enabled it to take its time to negotiate with lenders as well as provide some comfort to the lenders that the company could operate its business in normal course.

The professional fees associated with bankruptcy are potentially crushing and are another reason why companies hoard cash as they face financial difficulties. The debtor will need lawyers and financial advisors during a bankruptcy case. The debtors will typically be responsible for paying (contractually or by means of a carve-out or otherwise) the legal and financial advisors of each of their constituent committees. Retailers for whom reorganization or a *bona fide* going concern sale is a legitimate option want as much flexibility as possible while under the protection of the bankruptcy court, and so are especially incented to raise cash prior to a bankruptcy filing.

## Conclusion

The importance of cash and cash flow in the retail context cannot be overstated. Retailers need cash to justify their existence to their constituents, maintain a flow of fresh goods to satisfy the ever-fickle consumer base which votes with its feet every day, maintain leverage with those with whom it deals in the ordinary course and in the extraordinary environment of bankruptcy, and preserve as much flexibility as possible to navigate the shifting sands of the retail environment.

## E. Randall S. Eisenberg and Armen Emrikian — Prioritizing Liquidity During Difficult Times[15]

XYZ Company ("the Company") was a large manufacturer with abundant cash (approximately US\$500 million of cash on hand) and very profitable overseas operations, but was burdened with an uncompetitive labor contract and significant pension and post-retirement healthcare obligations in North America. The Company's restructuring was complicated, involving difficult negotiations with multiple stakeholders including customers, labor unions, and bondholders. The turbulence in the capital markets, softness in the general economy, and significant industry-specific declines further complicated the Company's efforts in achieving its restructuring objectives.

By the fall of 2006, the Company had depleted much of its cash war chest. The lender syndicate which had been comfortably secured throughout the case was seeing its collateral value diminish significantly, and began to exert leverage during negotiations by restricting additional access to funding and requiring permanent paydowns as the Company's borrowing base position deteriorated. The Company also had a concentrated customer base. Factoring companies began to deem significant customer receivables as ineligible due to credit risk considerations, and thus worked to ultimately limit their exposure to both the industry and the Company's customers.

Certain structural limitations posed challenges to the Company's ability to effectively manage liquidity during these challenging times. Like many publicly traded companies, XYZ historically focused on income statement-based metrics as a means to measure performance. Operating income as well as earnings before

---

[15]The opinions, facts, and conclusions contained herein are those of the authors or the sources cited and not those of FTI Consulting, Inc. The information contained herein is of a general nature and is not intended to address the circumstances of any particular individual, entity, or transaction. No one should act on such information without appropriate professional advice after a thorough examination of the particular situation.

interest, taxes, depreciation, amortization, and restructuring expense (EBITDAR) were typically used to measure performance and set incentive compensation targets. While certain cash flow items such as working capital and capital expenditures were forecast as part of the annual business planning process, the Company's divisions were focused on (and compensated for) earnings performance rather than cash flow performance.

The Company's labor situation in Europe, and to a lesser extent in the U.S., posed additional challenges toward managing liquidity. The Company had a vast footprint in Europe, with a heavy concentration in high-labor-cost countries such as France, Germany, and Portugal. Declining industry volumes had further depressed the profitability of the high-cost countries, and heightened the business case for downsizing operations and moving production to lower-cost countries in Eastern Europe. However, a significant limiting factor in executing such restructuring actions was the large, one-time severance liabilities arising from such actions. Due to limited liquidity in Europe, the Company was unable to invest in these actions.

The decentralized nature of the Company's European operations also posed challenges to managing liquidity. Approximately 25 legal entities were operating in multiple countries across Europe. Most of these legal entities reported to a single division and, as such, operated as stand-alone businesses focused on maximizing their earnings. The Company maintained a European cash-pooling system in Italy, whereby cash from the various European legal entities was consolidated once a month and disbursed to those entities in need of funding. Many cash-generating legal entities were preserving the use of their local financing lines for their local needs, thereby reducing the pool available to fund other entities.

Further frustrating the Company's tight liquidity situation in North America and Europe was the inability to routinely provide funding to these regions from its operations in the Asia-Pacific region, which was the Company's most cash flow-positive region. The Asia-Pacific region maintained cash in excess of that needed to fund operations, but was constrained in its ability to repatriate cash out of the region due to tight restrictions by foreign governments that limited dividend repatriation.

Initially, the goal was to understand the quality of cash flow forecasting in each region with an emphasis on North America and Europe. The two regions offered stark contrasts in forecasting methodology. The European operations were primarily housed in a single legal entity, with payables information aggregated in a centralized information system. Limited visibility existed into receipt-and-disbursement-basis cash flows by division, and thus operating divisions were not able to track their cash flows on this basis. As a result, the European cash flow forecast was highly centralized, with less detailed reporting on actual performance versus forecast performance.

North American cash flows were forecast individually at the legal entity level. The Company had an established methodology by which each legal entity forecast its cash flows over a six-month period. These cash flows were then reviewed by divisional management and consolidated by the regional treasury for purposes of generating a North American region cash flow forecast. Despite this process being in place for nearly 20 years, the analysis of actual performance versus historical forecasts illustrated significant shortcomings in forecasting accuracy at certain entities, along with limited ability to effectively explain variances of actual performance versus forecast performance.

Also of concern was the disconnectedness of the intercompany receipt/disbursement forecasts of the various entities. The Company maintained centralized support (e.g., sales, purchasing, and administrative) activities in a given region that supported multiple other regions. As a result, significant recurring intercompany billings were generated both within and across regions. However, after discussions with local management and analysis of intercompany activity in the cash flow forecasts, it became apparent that the various entities were not fully synchronized, both from absolute dollar and timing standpoints, in forecasting intercompany cash flows.

Based on these observations, management implemented more stringent controls and accountability in regional cash flow forecasting. The cash flow forecasting frequency was increased to weekly, with additional requirements to explain actual-to-forecast and forecast-to-forecast variances by division within each region. The balance of intercompany cash flows was closely evaluated in the forecast to ensure consistency both within and across regions. The increased forecast frequency, coupled with additional due diligence and questioning of the forecasts, led to noticeable improvements in forecast accuracy. In large part, this improvement was due to the increased visibility of divisional cash flows to both the working group and external stakeholders. This visibility provided the divisions motivation to improve forecast accuracy and reduce forecast conservatism, since a division did not want to be perceived as a cash drain which could lead to core versus non-core decisions.

XYZ had initiated a variety of financing and operating initiatives with the goal of minimizing cash burn and reaching cash flow breakeven in each region. The financing initiatives being pursued fell into two main categories. One main thrust was to maintain existing receivables financing capacity in North America in light of upcoming maturities on a large receivables line of credit. After negotiating a series of short maturity extensions, the Company was able to negotiate a replacement agreement with a new factoring company to mitigate the potential permanent loss of factoring capacity. While this was a key element in supporting North American liquidity, the replacement agreement only provided for financing on approximately 30 percent of total North American sales; therefore, further liquidity enhancement programs were needed.

The Company focused on identifying and implementing other financing support, including acceleration of customer receivables and improved management of intercompany accounts. The acceleration of customer receivables allowed the Company to effectively finance receivables which otherwise were ineligible to be factored. This also served to minimize receivable levels of potentially at-risk customers, though it should be noted that the Company was forced to pay overmarket prices for some of these temporary accelerations. Separately, the Company became more focused on managing payments across legal entities in various regions. Since the Company was a multi-billion dollar enterprise with functions housed in a given region supporting multiple regions, the intercompany netting process was one in which hundreds of millions of dollars were settled across regions in any given month. The Company analyzed month-end inter-company positions and identified opportunities to defer payment and/or accelerate receipt of intercompany amounts to assist in sup-porting cash-strapped regions. Given the relative size of the inter-company activity, the impact of managing the intercompany accounts served as the equivalent of an additional line of credit, particularly in the cash-strapped North American region.

The Company was also successful in monetizing several under-performing or non-operating assets. In mid-2007, management iden-tified all European past-due trade receivables which were not pledged as collateral in any of its bank facilities. After segregating those receivables management felt were collectible, the Company sold the remaining receivables on a non-recourse basis to a third-party collection agency for a recovery of 70–80 percent of face value. During the same time frame, management also sought opportu-nities to monetize tax receivables in certain European and Asian jurisdictions.

Financing options in Europe were virtually non-existent. In early 2007, the Company was suffering from widespread production shut-downs of its key customers leading to all-time low sales levels. Soon, the Company was faced with having to make a significant pay-down of its asset-based credit facility based on dramatically reduced receivables levels. Such a paydown would have significantly impaired liquidity since the Company had limited operating cash and all paydowns of its revolver were permanent reductions to the facility. Recognizing the consequences of a paydown, a mechanism was imple-mented to preserve the lenders' rights and to provide the Company continued access to these funds under certain conditions. The solu-tion was to have the amounts which were subject to paydown pre-funded into a cash collateral account. The funds in this cash collateral account would only be accessible to the Company if its borrowing base improved to levels which provided borrowing availability in excess of outstanding, thus allowing for the preservation of critical liquidity to support future working capital investment requirements when the industry situation began to improve.

Understanding the severity of the liquidity situation across most geographic regions, management actively began directing its divisions to develop and implement self-directed liquidity conservation measures immediately after the signals of a sharp drop in industry production volumes. While certain restructuring activities such as upfront cash outlays to reduce headcount and/or eliminate excess production capacity were centrally managed and required corporate approval, for the most part the divisions were deemed best suited to develop initiatives geared toward short-term cash conservation. Management confirmed that the divisions identified appropriate initiatives and had proper implementation plans in place to minimize cash burn during this period in which industry volumes were at unprecedented lows. In general, the initiatives of each division fell into the following categories: customer recovery, headcount initiatives, working capital, capital spending reductions, and vendor management.

Customer liquidity improvement actions were oriented around accelerated recoupment of upfront expenditures in support of new customer programs and the pursuit of customer payments and/or price increases to mitigate the impact of dramatic, unannounced changes in production schedules. While the Company set lofty goals for customer recovery, it was left swimming upstream against both a customer base which was saddled with its own liquidity problems as well as industry paradigms which considered supplier rescue a measure of last resort.

Headcount initiatives were another key element of the Company's liquidity initiatives. Permanent reductions of the labor force were enacted soon after the Company realized the severity of the industry downturn. Historically, the Company maintained a generous severance policy which would have resulted in significant upfront cash outlays to downsize the workforce to required levels. In order to execute the workforce downsizing within its liquidity constraints, two key changes were made to the severance policy: reducing the severance payout to six months (from one year), and modifying the payment timing such that payments would be stretched over a six-month period. Replicating this success in certain regions was more challenging due to the more stringent labor laws. However, being a significant employer in many foreign countries, the Company was able to successfully involve local governments in managing its labor costs. In certain countries, the Company was able to implement a four-day work week, while being reimbursed by the local government for employee pay on day 5. In other countries, the Company was able to generate significant employee participation in voluntary pay-as-you-go severance programs to avoid significant one-time outlays. The Company used the leverage of temporary layoffs (in which it was only required to pay employees a fraction of their total pay) as inducement to increase participation in its separation programs.

Working capital conservation was another key element of the Company's liquidity initiatives. Since the Company was unable to access its asset-based revolver for additional borrowings, managing accounts receivable collections and inventory purchasing was of utmost importance. Each of the divisions had well-organized processes for tracking and acting on past-due receivables. Contrary to traditional thinking of valuing the customer's future business much more than the customer's current business, the Company recognized the need to aggressively stay in front of all customers to ensure timely collection of receivables. In certain instances, the Corporate Treasurer and Chief Financial Officer (CFO) were actively involved in elevating significant past-due issues to similar levels at their customers and mandated "stop ships" to the extent the customer was not cooperative. Similarly, management's emphasis on liquidity conservation initiatives led to a noticeably increased emphasis on inventory management. Many of the divisions became much more active in downsizing material orders below levels projected, reducing re-order levels and quantities, reducing safety stock, and eliminating unnecessary touchpoints (e.g., intermediate warehouses) within the product value stream.

Another key element of the Company's liquidity initiatives was reduction and deferral of capital spending. The Company implemented a moratorium on non-customer program-specific capital spending almost immediately after widespread volume reduction announcements hit the market. However, this still left significant upcoming capital requirements to support upcoming customer program launches.

Vendor management was also essential to the Company's liquidity initiatives. In North America, the Company had historically purchased its primary raw material, scrap steel, through a single supplier. Due to the Company's financial condition and a desire to reduce its industry exposure, this vendor had dramatically reduced the Company's credit limit and demanded letters of credit for additional purchases beyond the credit limit. Given its bank's refusal to extend additional letters of credit, the Company was faced with a production interruption if it was not able to purchase scrap steel on comparable terms. The Company feverishly began to identify alternate vendors and develop a value proposition as to why these suppliers should provide credit on comparable terms to the incumbent supplier. The Company's primary leverage was the incremental purchasing volume it could provide the new suppliers. However, the potential new suppliers remained concerned with the industry condition and the Company's liquidity outlook. These suppliers undertook significant due diligence of the Company's business plan and short-term cash flow forecast to become comfortable with the idea of the Company as a new customer. During this period, the Company began to reduce its reliance on its existing supplier and gradually transitioned 100 percent of its scrap steel purchases from the existing supplier to two new suppliers at close to comparable pricing and terms.

Although the Company was focused on the right things and its liquidity initiatives were generally effective, key stakeholders continued to be very skeptical of the Company's cash conservation capabilities, particularly since the Company historically had limited transparency to its cash flow forecasting and liquidity initiatives outside of mandatory reporting requirements as per its credit agreement. As mentioned earlier, XYZ's Treasury department implemented a more frequent reporting cadence. This not only provided key stakeholders with more visibility into cash flow performance and forecasts in each main region, but it also elevated the accountability for cash flow improvement within the Company. As a result, divisional management — which was historically incentivized based on book income — was now further entrenched in managing short-term cash flow. This assisted in driving significantly improved cash flow performance throughout the Company.

While liquidity initiatives resulted in measurable improvements, North American cash flow remained negative primarily due to the inability of historical contractual unit pricing, which was established at normalized industry volume levels, to allow for profitable performance at volume levels which had been reduced by as much as 50 percent. Since it was critical to preserve scarce liquidity during this process, management focused on rapidly identifying immediate measures to further minimize cash burn above and beyond measures that had already been implemented. Certain measures, such as plant shutdowns, increased temporary layoff frequency, reduced direct material purchases, and freight consolidation, were implemented immediately. An additional list of contingent measures was developed (including, but not limited to, wage/headcount reductions, severance benefit reductions, and elimination of indirect spending) to allow for further savings in the short term.

Although the Company is not out of the woods yet, it has managed to maintain sufficient liquidity. This was accomplished through the recognition of liquidity conservation as a critical element of the Company's continued viability, along with management's ability to rapidly refocus and redirect the organization accordingly. Given the continued industry difficulties, the Company may find itself further delayed in resolving its situation to the satisfaction of its multiple stakeholders. Even if this is the case, as a result of placing liquidity conservation at the forefront of its management objectives, the Company has institutionalized the necessary cash flow management disciplines to make it better positioned for maximizing liquidity in the current economic downturn.

# F. Howard Brod Brownstein, CTP — Manage for Cash

There is an old saying that goes, "When you're up to your neck in alligators, it's difficult to remember that you came to drain the swamp." Managers who have been trained in business schools and on the job about how to maximize return on assets (ROA), return on investment (ROI), return on equity (ROE), or some other accounting-based measurement have too seldom also been taught about the importance of cash. Indeed, implicit in the notion that a company is healthy is an assumption that cash is *not* a problem — in fact, it is not even on anyone's radar screen.

Until relatively recently, the idea that major American companies could fail — in particular, the caliber of companies interviewing at leading business schools — was inconceivable. It was only the generation of business school students graduating in the 1990s that encountered widespread experience with corporate restructuring, albeit gained the hard way. So, the importance of "managing for cash", which grew out of the field of turnaround management, is still a relatively new idea, and is all too rarely taught as a mainstream concept in MBA programs.

Welcome to the post-Enron, post-WorldCom, post-financial meltdown era! The life cycle of businesses is increasingly seen not just in Darwinian terms of survival versus extinction, but as a *constant* struggle which, by its very nature, involves periodic strategic reconfiguration, financial and operational restructuring, and even regular re-examination of the business's economic justification to exist. Consulting firms abound that offer "change management", and popular bestsellers appear every few years preaching the importance of preparing for constant change.[16]

"Normal" can no longer realistically be expected to mean steady-state, predictable results. It seems like hubris to present *any* business plan, forecast, or projection, which extends to even the medium-term

---

[16]One of the author's favorites is Spencer Johnson's *Who Moved My Cheese? An Amazing Way to Deal with Change in Your Work and in Your Life*, G.P. Putnam's Sons, New York, 1998.

plan, without at least acknowledging the possibility — if not the likelihood — that the plan will have to be rethought, reconsidered, or wholly redone before the covered time period is completed. To forge ahead based upon the original plan alone is like steering a ship with sonar, but without an action-ready set of procedures for avoiding the unexpected obstacles and bad weather that invariably lay ahead. You may be fortunate enough to see the icebergs ahead, but you will not be able to avoid them!

It is hereby submitted that *every* business plan should be accompanied by a "Plan B" (or C, D, and E) which answers the question, "What if it don't?" If the future existence of the business is even remotely at stake, let alone if the underperformance of the business plan would materially affect the company's ability to operate or its valuation by the capital markets, then considering how the company manages for cash should be an integral part of *all* scenarios.

What does it mean to manage for cash? At the very least, it means to predict and measure the effect upon cash of every decision under consideration. Although cash is conventionally a balance sheet account, and therefore looked at as a static amount as of a certain date, it is *cash flow* that must be predicted, monitored, measured, and reported. So cash must be viewed as a liquid, not a solid.

One hears the most about managing for cash in the context of a turnaround. A business in distress can face imminent asphyxiation as stretched lines of credit from lenders and suppliers dry up, customers divert business when service levels drop and rumors fly about their supplier's future, and those employees who can leave — usually the best ones — do. The cows will not give and the hens will not lay. A once-proud business, often operated by founders or their descendants, is looking at annihilation.

This paradigm shift in management usually requires the presence of a turnaround professional who is well versed in the process of corporate renewal. Like the wagon train leaders who knew where to cross the rivers and how to negotiate with the Indians, the turnaround professional is a "temp", an interim advisor or manager who helps to steer the company through unfamiliar waters. The turnaround profession today boasts thousands of practitioners: some are "single shingle" experts; others are members of turnaround firms of varying sizes.

Yesterday's goals of increasing sales, market share, and profitability according to Generally Accepted Accounting Principles (GAAP) are immediately passé and must be shelved, as the turnaround professional knows that any chance for business survival requires a shift in focus to cash and cash alone. A "profitable" company that runs out of cash will be just as dead as an unprofitable one.

The turnaround professional's first hours and days on the job have been likened to triage in a hospital emergency room. For example, it is not unusual for the turnaround professional to discover shortly after his or her arrival that the client will likely miss payroll that very week — an urgent issue that had not been recognized by the client's management team. In fact, since many companies pay their employees one week in arrears, this turnaround effort is starting the race from about a mile *behind* the starting line!

Or, perhaps management had calmly assumed that their faithful lender would simply provide an overadvance loan without much fanfare, the same lender who had hosted golf outings and sumptuous dinners for years. In fact, that selfsame lender has become fed up by the company's mismanagement, and he is also worried about his own job. If the lender is a U.S.-based regulated depository institution, policies emanating from Washington, D.C. may effectively dictate the lender's refusal to take on more risk. The client's management has likely been in denial during the months or years leading up to this point, and may still be unprepared to face reality.

Therefore, the turnaround professional is, above all, a *reality merchant*, forcing the client to deal with the here and now. Notwithstanding that reliable data may be difficult to obtain, time is the enemy, and therefore much must be inferred very quickly from very little data. Turnaround professionals must deal with the harsh truth that they are being fed information by managers who, if they are not actively lying, may have no idea what the facts are but are afraid to admit it. Like battlefield surgeons, the turnaround professional must nonetheless take action *now*, since "not to decide is to decide".

Consider the case of a large fuel wholesaler in the Southwest USA. At the height of fuel's inflationary peak in mid-2008, the company's lenders understandably grew concerned. As is often the case with a rapid run-up in prices, gross margin dollars held steady but, as a percentage, margins had been cut in half. Spiraling prices would have spelled an increase in accounts receivable, even without the lengthening of the cash collection cycle which had resulted from customers facing pricing pressures and being unable to pay reliably as previously, and from refiners seeking faster payment in order to finance their own working capital needs. Financial leverage was therefore climbing precariously.

On paper, profits were up, which not only gave rise to celebration, but also led management to ignore how rapidly the company's cash was being dissipated. But profits are just an accounting measure, and a historical one at that. What the company needed was to focus on its current situation and its immediate future. Without decisive action recognizing the effect of recent events upon cash flow, the company would shortly run out of cash and was headed for disaster. Further borrowing was out of the question given the maxed-out leverage, and there was neither time nor receptive market conditions for raising equity. The company ironically would have filed bankruptcy on the same day it announced the highest "profits" in its history!

Fortunately, in this case, disaster was averted by decisive action focused on cash, led by an outside turnaround firm. The discipline of debt in this case had a salutary effect, because the company's lender required the company to engage a reputable turnaround firm or face imminent foreclosure. Like relatives staging an intervention with an alcoholic family member, the lender told the "credit-holic" borrower to "get help or else!" The lender presented a list of five turnaround firms with which the lender had previous experience, from which the borrower was to choose.

Understandably at first, the borrower was suspicious that these firms were just there to do the bank's bidding. Fortunately, the borrower's law firm had an active debtor-creditor law group, and its lead partner quickly assured the company's management that the turnaround firms listed by the lender were all reputable and qualified, and he was very familiar with at least three of them from prior experience. In particular, he recommended that the client engage a firm which included several Certified Turnaround Professionals (CTPs), a credential awarded by the Turnaround Management Association based upon, *inter alia*, at least five years' experience as a turnaround professional, passage of a rigorous examination, an extensive background check, and maintenance of continuing professional education. CTPs typically have made a career commitment to the turnaround profession, as contrasted with senior executives for whom turnaround consulting may be just a stopover between permanent jobs. Most importantly, CTPs adhere to a Code of Ethics which requires the exercise of independent judgment.

After a fast-track "beauty contest" of interviews of the three firms known to the borrower's law firm, the company selected a firm known for its focus on the middle market. The company's lawyer advised that the big-name national firms which were known for high-profile work with Fortune 100 companies would likely not commit their "A" team to a medium-sized company like the fuel wholesaler. The selected turnaround firm's case team was led by one of the firm's principals, so the borrower knew it was getting the turnaround firm's best resources.

The turnaround case team was a wonder to watch! Within hours, it had assembled a Management Action Team (MAT), leveraging the turnaround firm's expertise over a management team that had truly never encountered a situation like this before. In the face of scant data and pressures from multiple sources — the lender, the trade creditors, and the union — the turnaround case team systematically prioritized problems and dispatched solutions. Most notable was how the turnaround team *communicated.* The team let the lender know *immediately* about anything unfavorable and always coupled the news with steps being taken to deal with the situation. They advised the trade creditors of exactly what would happen if deliveries ceased, and how the trade creditors would fare in a crash-and-burn bankruptcy. Since many of the trade creditors were not familiar with the turnaround firm, they were provided with references to contact *at their own banks and law firms!* The turnaround case team negotiated quietly with the two largest suppliers and got them on board early in the process, and then the others simply followed suit. And throughout the entire process, one theme remained constant: the turnaround firm case team and the MAT managed for cash.

Once the immediate crisis was contained, with a 13-week rolling cash flow projection showing relative stability having been shared with all stakeholders, the MAT quickly implemented a plan to pass along the added working capital costs caused by slow-paying customers. Customer relationships of long standing were put on the line, but the rapidly shifting market conditions in the fuel industry fortunately favored the wholesaler with more negotiating power than it might otherwise have had. But at the end of the day, what enabled the company to survive was having recognized in time the importance of managing for cash.

While few turnarounds follow the same exact course, some recognizable phases are discernible that many turnarounds follow: Management Change, Situation Analysis, Emergency Action, Business Restructuring, and Return to Normalcy.[17] These phases do not occur sequentially, but rather may be overlapping, telescoping one into the other.

During the Management Change phase, a virtual transformation must occur in the day-to-day purpose of business activities — i.e., the importance of managing for cash must be recognized, and decision making must begin and end with the effect upon cash. Cash is like oxygen to a company in turnaround mode, and, like the danger of permanent brain damage to a patient with anoxia, the speed with which managing for cash is instituted is critical. Since the pre-existing management team will typically not be schooled in turnaround management, the Management Change phase will include engagement of a turnaround professional and assembly of an MAT. In some cases, the turnaround professional will function as a hands-on manager of the company, such as in the role of Chief Restructuring Officer

---

[17]Based upon a "turnaround matrix" authored by Thomas D. Hays III, CTP, and used in connection with review courses in preparation for the CTP examination.

or Interim CEO. In other cases, the turnaround professional is in an advisory role, but is counted upon to make sure that needed changes actually occur. During the Management Change phase, the turnaround professional will open lines of communication with key stakeholders, such as lenders, trade creditors, unions, etc., in order to obtain their input into the process and to keep tabs on how each is feeling and what action each may be contemplating. The filing of involuntary bankruptcies by disgruntled trade creditors is nearly always the result of lack of communication.

Early in the process, the Situation Analysis phase will also begin, during which the current cash flow trajectory is identified, utilizing a rolling 13-week cash flow projection. How soon will the company run out of cash? What are the factors — cash inflows and outflows — that are influencing this trajectory? What needs to be done *now* to prevent "game over" (exhaustion of the company's cash flow)? Just as the analysis of a chess game requires a threshold determination of whether the opponent can put you in check or win a piece, the initial focus in Situation Analysis is to manage for cash.

The Situation Analysis phase also begins with a viability assessment: "Is there a pony under the pile of manure?" What are the strategic alternatives available, and what are the risks and resources attendant to each alternative? The fact is, *any* company can be turned around, regardless of how dire its condition, provided that an unlimited amount of time and money are available.

Since those conditions can never be met, the real questions will be: What will the turnaround process cost? How long will it take? What are the risks that it will not be successful, or that the result will be a company which is too weak to withstand market and other pressures? As much as the shareholder may wish for a turnaround, the resources to fund the effort may not be available. In a way, "turnaround" management is a misnomer, and "optimization" management — achieving the best practical result under the circumstances — may be a more accurate label. As difficult as it may be for some to accept, the optimal outcome may be a sale of all or part of the business, or liquidation. Inasmuch as officers and directors of a distressed business in the zone of insolvency have a fiduciary duty to consider the interests of creditors, such unattractive outcomes must nonetheless be considered.

During the turnaround professional's early days on the job, his or her role may have to be revised if he or she determines that management is nonfeasant, or worse. Stakeholders may have lost trust in the company's management, and the situation may therefore be improved by the appointment of a Chief Restructuring Officer who can restore credibility and obtain needed creditor and lender support.

Emergency Action will also likely begin on day 1 and take more shape as the Situation Analysis proceeds. Payrolls must be met, utilities must be paid, and vendors must be dealt with. There may be an imminent decision needed about whether to file bankruptcy, requiring analysis about the company's suitability for a debtor-in-possession (DIP) loan or cash collateral agreement with its lender. Nevertheless, managing for cash remains the order of the day, as most (if not all) Emergency Actions will be focused on improving cash flow. Accounts receivable and collections will be given heightened attention — possibly for the first time — as customers are offered late and/or enhanced prompt payment discounts, and receive calls in advance of due dates for substantial payments. A shift to selling on the basis of cash in advance (CIA) or cash on delivery (COD) will be considered, as well as obtaining advance deposits for special orders or sole-source contracts. Vendors will be contacted and accounts payable stretched, possibly with an informal mini-restructuring involving the terming-out of existing amounts owed. Open communication channels will be maintained with all stakeholders whose unfavorable actions could worsen the company's situation: lenders, creditors, unions, etc.

Before very long, the outcomes analysis described above will have resulted in a vision of what the company should look like in the future, assuming it is not going to be sold or liquidated, and the phase of Business Restructuring will begin. Since it would accomplish little to restore the company to exactly the position it was in before the problems occurred, only to have those or similar problems recur, Business Restructuring incorporates confirmation that the root causes of the company's distress have been adequately addressed. During Business Restructuring, the concept of profitability is reintroduced, but as just one metric and not as a mantra. In the long term, the company will of course have to be profitable, have sustainable market share, and earn an acceptable return on its assets in order to justify its economic existence. However, successful restructuring will also require the establishment of systems and controls that are geared toward managing for cash, so that the company does not get into cash trouble again.

Finally, if the resources were available and the risks were reasonable such that the turnaround process has been successful, the company can plan to Return to Normalcy. Profitable growth can be resumed and long-term strategies, including acquisitions and resort to the capital markets, can be considered. Presumably, the business will have a clearer picture of its economic model and how to maintain its market franchise. But the company's brush with death should never be forgotten, and this vigilance should be expressed in terms of rigorous measurements that require the company to always manage for cash.

# 17. Biographies
# of Contributors

## Howard Brod Brownstein, CTP

Howard Brownstein is a nationally known turnaround and crisis management professional. He is the President of The Brownstein Corporation, which provides turnaround management and advisory services to companies and their stakeholders, as well as investment banking services, fiduciary services, and litigation consulting, investigation and valuation services. He was previously a Founding Principal of NachmanHaysBrownstein, Inc. where, in addition to leading turnaround assignments for its clients (advising senior management or fulfilling a senior management role), he had overall responsibility for the firm's transactional activities and for the marketing of its services to clients.

Mr. Brownstein recently served as Chief Restructuring Officer in *U.S. Mortgage*, which involved a US$138 million mortgage fraud; and led the Plan Administrator team in *Montgomery Ward LLC*, the largest retail liquidation in history. He served on the Board of Directors of Special Metals Corporation, a US$1 billion nickel alloy producer where he also chaired the Audit Committee and which was sold in 2006 at a substantial gain, and on the Board of Directors of Magnatrax Corporation, a US$500 million manufacturer of metal buildings that was similarly sold in 2007. He has served as Financial Advisor to debtors and to lenders and creditor committees in bankruptcy proceedings; and as a litigation expert in several cases, including the landmark *Merry-Go-Round* bankruptcy.

Howard Brownstein serves as Chair of the Board of Trustees of the National Philanthropic Trust, which is among the fastest-growing charities and largest grant-making institutions nationally (over US$1 billion to date) as well as the largest independent provider of donor-advised funds in the U.S. (with over US$700 million under management).

Previously, Mr. Brownstein was Managing Director of Enprotech Corporation, a wholly owned subsidiary of ITOCHU (formerly C. Itoh), one of the world's largest companies. Enprotech acted as ITOCHU's acquisition and holding company for engineering service and product businesses with over US$1 billion in assets. Mr. Brownstein has served in several senior executive and board positions, including CEO and COO of The Stone Group, a leading multinational manufacturer of comfort and safety equipment for the passenger rail industry, with operations in the United States, Spain, and England. Prior to becoming a turnaround management consultant, Mr. Brownstein also served on the board of a regional bank and founded a metals trading firm.

Mr. Brownstein is a Certified Turnaround Professional (CTP). He has served on the International Board of Directors of the Turnaround Management Association (TMA) and its Executive Committee, and chaired its Audit Committees. Mr. Brownstein received the TMA's "Outstanding Individual Contribution" award in 2007. He is also a member of the Board of the American Bankruptcy Institute (ABI) and co-chairs its Mid-Atlantic region, and serves on the Governing Board of the Commercial Finance Association's (CFA) Education Foundation. Mr. Brownstein is a frequent speaker at professional and educational programs, including at Harvard Business School, Villanova Law School, Northeastern University, ABI, the American Bar Association, and TMA. He has authored over 30 articles, and has served on the Editorial Board of *The Journal of Corporate Renewal* and currently serves as a Contributing Editor of *ABF Journal*.

Howard Brownstein is a graduate of Harvard University, where he obtained JD and MBA degrees, and of the University of Pennsylvania, where he obtained BS and BA degrees from the Wharton School and the College of Arts and Sciences. Mr. Brownstein is admitted to the bars of Pennsylvania, Massachusetts, and Florida, but does not actively practice law. He also served in the U.S. Air Force Reserve, attaining the rank of First Lieutenant in the Medical Service Corps.

## Michael Chartock

Michael Chartock is a Principal and Managing Director of Gordon Brothers Group, a global advisory, restructuring, and investment firm specializing in retail and consumer products as well as in the industrial and real estate sector. Mr. Chartock is an expert in sourcing, structuring, and overseeing complex dispositions, particularly retail and real estate store closings and wind-downs outside of bankruptcy. Mr. Chartock regularly works with multiple corporate constituencies in connection with consensual out-of-court compositions and wind-downs, strong parent companies wishing to dispose of their underperforming retail subsidiaries, and healthy retailers in connection with their ordinary course store relocations and closings. Prior to joining Gordon Brothers Group in 1999, he practiced corporate law for over 10 years, including as Senior Counsel at Harcourt General/The Neiman Marcus Group. Mr. Chartock received his BA from Brandeis University and his JD from Cornell Law School, and has served as Vice President and Board Member of the International Turnaround Management Association.

## Randall S. Eisenberg

Randall S. Eisenberg is a Senior Managing Director in FTI's Corporate Finance practice and is based in New York. Mr. Eisenberg co-leads FTI's services to underperforming companies. He has extensive experience advising senior management, boards of directors, and equity sponsors in revitalizing companies that are stagnant, underperforming, or in crisis. Mr. Eisenberg has led many large, high-profile national and international assignments.

# Armen Emrikian

Armen Emrikian is a Managing Director in FTI's Corporate Finance practice and is based in Chicago. For the past eight years, Mr. Emrikian has provided corporate financial, strategic, and restructuring advisory services to companies and their creditors in a variety of industries, including automotive, light industrial, retail, telecommunications, and independent power production.

# Kenneth B. Furry

Kenneth B. Furry is Counsel at Realization Services, Inc. Mr. Furry has more than 26 years of experience as a legal advisor to both publicly traded and privately owned companies. Mr. Furry has practiced extensively in the general corporate, commercial, regulatory, and transactional areas. His background includes mergers and acquisitions, secured loan transactions, restructuring of troubled companies, settling of employment and ownership disputes, negotiation and structuring of complex commercial agreements, and joint ventures. Mr. Furry was Counsel in the Manhattan office of Parker Chapin LLP (now Troutman Sanders LLP). He also served for six years as Vice President and Counsel at a New York Stock Exchange-listed financial institution, where he handled securities, regulatory, and compliance matters, and acted as primary legal advisor for real estate lending, leasing, and other business units. Mr. Furry received his BS, MBA, and JD degrees from Cornell University.

# Michael F. Gries

Michael Gries is Co-Founder of Conway Del Genio Gries & Co. LLC and is a nationally recognized leader in the restructuring profession, with more than 25 years' experience advising companies and creditors on complex corporate reorganizations. Over the course of his career, he has been responsible for a myriad of restructurings, divestitures, and acquisitions — representing companies, lenders, and bondholders — that included valuation, strategic assessment, overhead reduction initiatives, business plan development and evaluation, capital raising, and negotiation. Mr. Gries has overseen engagements in a broad range of industries, including aerospace, apparel and textile design and marketing, automotive, construction and engineering, distribution, electrical contracting, energy services, gaming, health care, manufacturing, mechanical contracting, mining, publishing and media, power generation, real estate, retail, shipbuilding, technology, trading, and transportation.

Mr. Gries has gained a stellar reputation as an expert witness, having testified in over 10 trials and countless depositions encompassing transaction and stand-alone valuation, divestiture strategy and valuation in distressed sales, sources and uses of funds, as well as numerous matters related to the requirements under Chapter 11 of the U.S. Bankruptcy Code (including events leading to the filing, financing, divestitures, retention plans, and strategic direction).

Mr. Gries received his BS in Business Administration, with a Major in Accounting, from Northeastern University. Mr. Gries is a Certified Public Accountant and a Certified Restructuring and Reorganization Accountant.


## Michael P. Healy

Michael Healy is a Vice President at Conway Del Genio Gries & Co. LLC (CDG), and focuses on corporate restructurings and mergers and acquisitions. His experience encompasses a variety of industries, including healthcare, retail, and finance. Prior to joining CDG, Mr. Healy worked for Northeast Capital & Advisory, Inc. in its Merger & Acquisition Advisory and Capital Financing departments. He holds a BS in Business Management from Rensselaer Polytechnic Institute, as well as an MBA in Finance from the Lally School of Management and Technology.


## Julie H. Hertenstein

Julie H. Hertenstein is an Associate Professor of Accounting and the Sam and Nancy Altschuler Research Fellow at Northeastern

University, and a Senior Research Fellow with the Design Management Institute. She received her DBA and MBA degrees from Harvard University, and her BS from The Ohio State University. Her research focuses on the influence of financial and non-financial information on the development and success of new products. She also publishes and conducts research on discussion teaching effectiveness and student learning. Dr. Hertenstein's articles appear in leading journals, including *Management Accounting, Journal of Product Innovation Management, Advances in Management Accounting, Business Horizons, Design Management Journal, Case Research Journal, Communication Education*, and *Journal on Excellence in College Teaching*. She has written numerous cases published in leading accounting textbooks. She previously held information technology management positions at Pacific Telephone and Burlington Industries.

# Barry L. Kasoff

Barry L. Kasoff is President of Realization Services, Inc., a management consulting firm located in Bedford Hills, New York. A turnaround management expert in both financial and operating systems, Mr. Kasoff is the most certified professional in finance and accounting worldwide. He holds 14 professional certifications, as well as two MBA degrees from New York University's Stern School of Business (in Accounting and Information Systems). Mr. Kasoff is licensed in four states as a Certified Public Accountant (CPA), and has authored numerous book reviews for the *Journal of Accountancy* (published by The American Institute of Certified Public Accountants).

Mr. Kasoff's certifications include the following (among others): Chartered Financial Analyst; Certified Management Accountant; Certified Internal Auditor; Certified Turnaround Professional; Certified Insolvency and Reorganization Advisor; Certified Financial Manager; Certified Fraud Examiner; Certified Computing Professional; Certified Forensic Consultant; and Diplomat of the American Board of Forensic Accounting.

Mr. Kasoff was General Manager of Takarajimasha, a Japanese communications conglomerate, for six years. He identified and evaluated its investments and supervised the company's U.S.- and European-based operations. Fluent in Japanese business practices, Mr. Kasoff managed communications with Takarajimasha's Japanese parent company and directed the disposition of four companies and the consolidation of West Coast operations to the East Coast.

Prior to Takarajimasha, Mr. Kasoff was Vice President of Operations with the Selzer Group, a New York-based investment banking and leveraged buyout group comprised of public and private companies. Selzer had total revenues in excess of US$500 million. Mr. Kasoff identified and implemented improvements in cost structures, control, and financial reporting throughout the Group's subsidiaries.

Before joining Selzer, Mr. Kasoff served as Director of Special Projects for CBS Publishing, a US$300 million corporation. At CBS, he analyzed business units, made recommendations for continued investment or disposition of business units (core businesses), and assisted in establishing an investment management process. At CBS, Inc., Mr. Kasoff reported directly to the Board of Directors, assisting in the revision of the company's hurdle rate. He also evaluated acquisitions and dispositions.


## Wendy Landon

Wendy Landon serves as the Portfolio Manager of distressed and secondary debt investments at GB Merchant Partners LLC. Ms. Landon has over 17 years' experience investing in distressed and high-yield markets, and has focused on the retail and consumer industries as well as on the media and telecommunications industries. Ms. Landon has sat on creditors' committees and has served on boards of directors, including at Samuels Jewelers and Smith & Hawken. Ms. Landon started her career at Fidelity Investments and then at DDJ Capital Management LLC, where she was an Assistant Portfolio Manager for high-yield funds and managed accounts. Ms. Landon received her BS in Economics and her MBA from the Wharton School of the University of Pennsylvania.

# Marjorie B. Platt

Marjorie B. Platt is Group Coordinator and Professor of Accounting at Northeastern University. She received her PhD and MA from the University of Michigan, her MBA from Babson College, and her BA from Northwestern University. She is a Certified Management Accountant (CMA). A Senior Research Fellow with the Design Management Institute, her current research focuses on how managers use financial and non-financial information in the process of making business decisions, particularly those that deal with new product design and development and the evaluation of design performance. In addition, she publishes and consults on the prediction of corporate bankruptcy and financial distress. Her most recent articles have appeared in *Journal of Product Innovation Management, Advances in Management Accounting, Design Management Journal Academic Review, Accounting Horizons, Case Research Journal, Journal of Business Research, Journal of Business Finance & Accounting,* and *Journal of Banking and Finance.*

# Baker Smith, CTP

Baker Smith is a Managing Director of BDO Consulting Corporate Advisors and has over 25 years' experience in crisis management, turnaround planning, and strategic advice to company owners, management, lenders, creditors, and investors. Mr. Smith has led over 200 crisis management and turnaround teams for distressed companies, ranging from US$25 million to several billion dollars in revenues, several as interim CEO and Chief Restructuring Officer (CRO). High-profile assignments have included interim CEO of Pic 'N Pay Stores, Inc. (453 stores in 23 states), Bank Syndicate Advisor for General Time (Westclox, Baby Ben), Financial Advisor to The Athlete's Foot, and Turnaround Advisor to Dixon Ticonderoga. Mr. Smith has previously served as a Principal with MorrisAnderson & Associates. He is Vice President of the Turnaround Management Association (TMA) and Past-President of the Association of Certified Turnaround Professionals. His education includes a BS from the U.S. Naval Academy, an MBA from Northeastern University, a JD from Suffolk University, and an LLM from Georgetown University. He is a member of the Beta Gamma Sigma business honor society. Mr. Smith has received the TMA's "Outstanding Contribution to the Turnaround Profession" award. He is a Certified Turnaround Professional (CTP). Mr. Smith holds a Certificate in Family Business Advising with Fellow Status. He is a member of the TMA, American Bankruptcy Institute (ABI), and Association of Corporate Growth (ACG), and is a prolific author.

# Index